SWIPE
TO UNLOCK

SWIPE
TO UNLOCK

The Primer on Technology and
Business Strategy

Neel Mehta
Aditya Agashe
Parth Detroja

Swipe to Unlock
Copyright © 2019, 2018, 2017 Belle Applications, Inc.
Published by Belle Applications, Inc.
swipetounlock.com

3rd Edition, 4th Revision (November 2019)

ISBN-13: 978-1976182198
ISBN-10: 1976182190

To my friends for their constant inspiration, and my family for being my rock — Neel

To my family and friends, thanks for supporting my passion for business and helping me push past my fears to embrace entrepreneurship — Adi

To my friends and family for their never-ending support, and my mentor Deborah Streeter for believing in my vision, which helped make this book possible — Parth

When you grow up, you tend to get told that the world is the way it is and your life is just to live your life inside the world, try not to bash into the walls too much, try to have a nice family, have fun, save a little money. That's a very limited life. Life can be much broader, once you discover one simple fact, and that is that everything around you that you call life was made up by people that were no smarter than you. And you can change it, you can influence it, you can build your own things that other people will use... That's maybe the most important thing. It's to shake off this erroneous notion that life is there and you're just gonna live in it, versus embrace it, change it, improve it, make your mark upon it... Once you learn that, you'll never be the same again.

— **Steve Jobs**
(who, by the way, never wrote any code for Apple)

Contents

Introduction

No matter what you do for a living, it's become essential to understand technology. Doctors are now using artificial intelligence to diagnose patients.[1] Farmers are using drones to grow better crops.[2] Businesspeople have realized that, while the world's biggest companies used to be oil and electric firms,[3] they're now the likes of Apple, Amazon, Facebook, Google, and Microsoft.[4]

So, how do you learn to understand technology?

It often feels like you have to be a master coder to understand the barrage of concepts that techies talk about: SaaS, APIs, SSL, cloud computing, and augmented reality, to name a few. And it often feels like you have to have an MBA to make sense of the daily deluge of tech news: startups, acquisitions, app launches, rumors, you name it.

But we think anyone can understand tech, no matter their background. We think the most important technology topics — from the nuts and bolts of the internet to the business strategies of Facebook and Uber — can be explained in plain, simple English.

The goal

Swipe to Unlock is a primer on technology and business strategy. In this book, we'll use real-world examples to break down the software, hardware, and business strategies that power the tech world and give you the tools to start understanding, analyzing, and shaping tech yourself. No prior knowledge is assumed.

Each section in *Swipe to Unlock* is a real-world case study, posing a question you might have had yourself — like how Spotify recommends songs, how self-driving cars work, and why Amazon offers free shipping with Prime even though it loses them money.

In each section, we'll explain the *what* — the technology concepts like big data and machine learning — and then the *why* — the business reasons why companies would use these technologies in the first place. We'll draw on our experience working as product managers at tech companies large and small to give you insights into how the world of tech operates.

By the end of this book, we aim to unlock your ability to think like a technologist. We'll train you to think through tech topics you encounter in the future: how the technology works, why it was made that way, where the money comes from, and whether or not it'll succeed. While specific apps and companies come and go, we hope that the core concepts you'll learn in *Swipe to Unlock* will be useful for a long time to come.

Who this book is for

Swipe to Unlock aims to be accessible to people of all skill levels. Whether you're a casual observer or a business professional, we think you'll find something useful and interesting.

If you don't have a coding background but want to break into product management, business development, marketing, or other non-engineering roles at tech companies, you'll have to be able to explain things like artificial intelligence, algorithms, and big data to teammates and clients. And to shape your company's business strategies you'll have to know which business strategies have been successful (or not) in the past and why. *Swipe to Unlock*'s case studies and plain-English explanations of tech concepts should help you with both.

If you're a software engineer but want to move toward product management roles, we'll teach you about the business side of the equation: ads, monetization, acquisitions, and the like.

If you're an entrepreneur or a tech leader, you know it's not enough to just build a great product. We'll use real-world case studies to build up your understanding of tech and intuition of business strategy so you can figure out how to make your company thrive and speak intelligently with investors and employees.

If you're a student of tech and business, *Swipe to Unlock*'s case studies will fit right in with your classes. You'll learn what has made companies like Amazon succeed and why products like Blackberry failed, and you'll get a feel for how tech companies have handled tech policy, disruption, and emerging markets.

Even if you don't work at a tech company, chances are your company can use tech to stay ahead of the curve. Predictive analytics, software-as-a-service, A/B testing — you'll learn about these hot terms and how even non-tech companies have used them to grow their businesses.

Finally, even if you don't need to know tech for your career, you still use it every day — you probably have an advanced piece of technology in your pocket right now. We'll help you become a better-informed digital citizen by using analogies and plain English to explain how the tech you use every day works. We'll also cover topics you might have heard on the news, such as net neutrality, privacy, and tech regulation. We'll even look at the dark side of tech: fake news, data breaches, digital drug trafficking, and robot-powered job destruction.

No matter why you're reading *Swipe to Unlock*, we think you'll find plenty of valuable insights and ideas, and you'll learn how to think — and speak! — like a technologist.

Before we dive in, let's take a look at what you'll be reading about.

What's inside

Swipe to Unlock is broken into three big chunks. The first chunk, chapters 1 to 4, breaks down the fundamentals of technology: how software is built, how the internet works, and the business models of major apps. The second chunk, chapters 5 through 8, gives you a tour of the tech world's major components: big data, cloud computing, security, and the like. The third chunk, chapters 9 to 12, builds off the first two and dives deep into trends, analysis, and predictions: business strategy, emerging markets, tech policy, and what's next in technology.

Each chapter builds off the previous ones, so if you're new to technology we recommend reading *Swipe to Unlock* front-to-back. If you're more seasoned, feel free to jump around to whatever cases seem the most relevant — each case can be read independently if you've learned the necessary concepts.

After the main content, we've included a glossary of the most important terms we've come across while working in the tech industry, covering programming languages, business jargon, common software engineering tools, and more. We think it'll help you speak like a technologist and be a useful reference for you going forward.

Finally, we couldn't possibly cover everything about tech and business strategy in a single book, so we've provided hundreds of citations per chapter. You'll find these links on our website at swipetounlock.com/notes/3.4.0. We encourage you to use the citations to dive deeper into any topic that interests you!

Who we are

When the three of us first met, we started talking about how Silicon Valley, for all its talk about openness and meritocracy, actually makes it quite hard for non-experts to understand it, let alone break into the tech industry. We realized we were passionate about changing that — which is why we wrote *Swipe to Unlock*.

The three of us have all worked as product managers at major tech companies, but we come from very different parts of the tech world — Neel from the public and nonprofit sectors, Adi from the startup space, and Parth from the business and marketing side. We hope our combined perspectives and insights prove useful for you.

Here's a bit more about us.

Neel Mehta is a Product Manager at Google. He previously worked at Microsoft, Khan Academy, and the US Census Bureau, where he launched the first fully-funded tech internship program in the federal government. He graduated *cum laude* from Harvard University.

Aditya Agashe is a Product Manager at Microsoft. Previously, he was the founder and CEO of Belle Applications. He graduated *cum laude* from Cornell University.

Parth Detroja is a Product Manager at Facebook. He has previously worked at Microsoft, Amazon, and IBM as a product manager and marketer. He graduated *summa cum laude* from Cornell University.

Notes for job hunters

Before we get started, we have some tips and resources for you if you're looking for a non-engineering role at a tech company.

First, bear in mind that the questions we'll answer in *Swipe to Unlock* aren't designed to resemble actual interview questions, but they will give you the technical and business insights to craft answers that'll set you apart from the pack.

For instance, in *Swipe to Unlock* we'll cover how Google decides what ads to show people and why Microsoft bought LinkedIn. Interviewers probably won't ask you to regurgitate these cases, but they might ask you how to increase ad revenue from a particular demographic or how to improve Microsoft's enterprise products — in which case, these cases will help you give more insightful answers and show the depth of your industry knowledge.

Swipe to Unlock, in other words, is focused on training you to think like a technologist instead of teaching you how to interview. Sample interview questions alone won't help you think strategically about the tech industry or become fluent in tech concepts, but we think *Swipe to Unlock* will.

For more tactical advice on preparing for interviews, creating a resume, networking, and choosing a job, check out swipetounlock.com/resources, where we share links to some useful books and articles.

Thank you!

Whatever your personal, academic, or career goals, we hope *Swipe to Unlock* proves useful for you. Thank you again for choosing to read *Swipe to Unlock*, and we hope you enjoy!

Neel Mehta
namehta.com
linkedin.com/in/neelmehta18

Aditya Agashe
adityaagashe.com
linkedin.com/in/adityaagashe
quora.com/profile/Adi-Agashe

Parth Detroja
parthdetroja.com
linkedin.com/in/parthdetroja

Chapter 1.
Software Development

Let's start our exploration of the world of technology by looking under the hood of the apps you use every day. Netflix and Microsoft Excel might feel pretty different, but they're both made from the same building blocks. In fact, we'd argue that every app is made from these same building blocks. What are they? Read on.

How does Google search work?

Whenever you search on Google, the search engine combs through the over 30 trillion webpages on the internet and finds the top 10 results for your question.[1] 92% of the time, you'll click on a result on the first page (that is, among the top 10 results).[2] Finding the top 10 things out of 30 trillion is really hard — it's about as hard as trying to find a penny randomly dropped somewhere in New York City.[3] Yet Google does this expertly and in just half a second, on average.[4] But how?

Google doesn't actually visit every page on the internet every time you ask it something. Google actually stores information about webpages in databases (tables of information, like in Excel), and it uses algorithms that read those databases to decide what to show you. Algorithms are just series of instructions — humans might have an "algorithm" to make a PB&J sandwich, while Google's computers have algorithms to find webpages based on what you typed into the search bar.

Crawling

Google's algorithm starts by building a database of every webpage on the internet. Google uses programs called spiders to "crawl" over webpages until it's found all of them (or at least, what Google thinks is all of them). The spiders start on a few webpages and add those to Google's list of pages, called the "index." Then, the spiders follow all the outgoing links on those pages and find a new set of pages, which they add to the index. Next, they follow all the links on *those* pages, and so on, until Google can't find anything else.

This process is always ongoing; Google is always adding new pages to its index or updating pages when they change. The index is huge, weighing in at over 100 million gigabytes.[5] If you tried to fit that on one-terabyte external hard drives, you'd need 100,000 — which, if you stacked them up, would be around a mile high.[6]

Word search

When you search Google, it grabs your query (the text you typed into the search bar) and looks through its index to find the webpages that are most relevant.

How might Google do this? The simplest way would be to just look for occurrences of a particular keyword, kind of like hitting Ctrl+F or Cmd+F to search a giant Word document. Indeed, this is how search engines in the 90's used to work: they'd search for your query in their index and show the pages that had the most matches,[7] an attribute called keyword density.[8]

This turned out to be pretty easy to game. If you searched for the candy bar Snickers, you'd imagine that snickers.com would be the first hit. But if a search engine just counted the number of times the word "snickers" appeared on a webpage, anyone could make a random page that just said "snickers snickers snickers snickers" (and so on) and jump to the top of the search results. Clearly, that's not very useful.

PageRank

Instead of keyword density, Google's core innovation is an algorithm called PageRank, which its founders Larry Page and

Sergey Brin created for their PhD thesis in 1998.[9] Page and Brin noticed that you can estimate a webpage's importance by looking at which other important pages link to them.[10] It's like how, at a party, you know someone is popular when they're surrounded by *other* popular people. PageRank gives each webpage a score that's based on the PageRank scores of every other page that links to that page.[11] (The scores of *those* pages depend on the pages that link to them, and so on; this gets calculated with linear algebra.[12])

For instance, if we made a brand-new webpage about Abraham Lincoln, it would initially have very low PageRank. If some obscure blog added a link to our page, our page would get a small boost to its PageRank. PageRank cares more about the quality of incoming links rather than the quantity,[13] so even if dozens of obscure blogs linked to our page, we wouldn't gain much. But if a New York Times article (which probably has a high PageRank) linked to our page, our page would get a huge PageRank boost.

Once Google finds all the pages in its index that mention your search query, it ranks them using several criteria, including PageRank.[14] Google has many other criteria as well: it considers how recently a webpage was updated, ignores websites that look spammy (like the "snickers snickers snickers snickers" site we mentioned earlier), considers your location (it could return the NFL if you search for "football" in the US, but the English Premier League if you search for "football" in England), and more.[15]

Gaming Google?

There are pitfalls to PageRank, however. Much like spammers abused keyword density (as with "snickers snickers snickers snickers"), spammers have now started making "link farms," or webpages that contain tons of unrelated links. Website owners can pay link farms to include a link to their webpages, which would artificially boost their PageRank.[16] However, Google has gotten pretty good at catching and ignoring link farms.[17]

There are some more mainstream ways to game Google, though. An entire industry, called search engine optimization (SEO), has sprung up to help website owners crack Google's search algorithm and make sure their webpages appear at the top of Google searches.[18] The most basic form of SEO is getting more pages to link to your page. SEO includes plenty more techniques, such as putting the right keywords in your page's title and headings or making all of your site's pages link to each other.[19]

Google's search algorithm is always changing, though; Google rolls out minor updates over 500 times a year.[20] There are occasionally more major updates, and after each, SEO experts try to find ways to use the changes to get ahead. For instance, Google changed its algorithm in 2018 to favor websites that loaded faster on mobile devices, leading experts to suggest that website owners make stripped-down articles with a Google tool called Accelerated Mobile Pages, or AMP.[21]

How does Spotify recommend songs to you?

Every Monday morning, Spotify sends its listeners a playlist of 30 songs that are, almost magically, perfectly tuned to their tastes. This playlist, called Discover Weekly, was an instant hit: within six months of launching in June 2015, it was streamed over 1.7 billion times.[22] But how does Spotify get to know its 200 million users so intimately?[23]

Spotify does employ music experts who hand-curate public playlists,[24] but there's no way they could do that for all 200 million Spotify users. Instead, Spotify has turned to an algorithm they run every week.[25]

The Discover Weekly algorithm starts by looking at two basic pieces of information. First, it looks at all the songs you've listened to and liked enough to add to your library or playlists. It's even smart enough to know that if you skipped a song within the first 30 seconds, you probably didn't like it. Second, it looks at all the playlists that other people have made, with the assumption that every playlist has some thematic connection; for instance, you could have a "running" playlist or a "Beatles jam" playlist.[26]

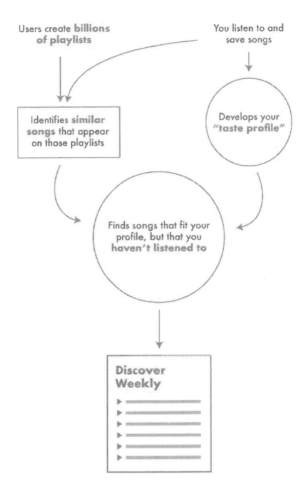

Spotify's algorithm for automatically recommending songs for you.
Source: Quartz[27]

Once it has this data, Spotify uses two methods to find songs you might like. The first method involves comparing the two datasets to figure out which new songs are related to the ones you like. For instance, suppose someone made a playlist with eight songs on it, and seven of those are in your library. You probably like this type of song, so Discover Weekly might recommend the one song that isn't in your library.[28]

This technique is called "collaborative filtering," and it's the same technique that Amazon uses to suggest items you might like based on your purchase history and the purchases of millions of other users.[29] Netflix's movie suggestions, YouTube's video suggestions, and Facebook's friend suggestions also use collaborative filtering.[30]

Collaborative filtering gets more and more useful as a service gets more users — in this case, when there are more Spotify users, it's easier to find someone with similar tastes to a particular person, and hence easier to make a recommendation. But these algorithms can get slow and computationally-intensive as their user base grows, too.[31]

The second method that Spotify uses to make your playlist is your "taste profile." Based on just the songs you've listened to and liked, Spotify will determine which genres (e.g. indie rock or R&B) and micro-genres (e.g. chamber pop or New Americana) you like and recommend songs from those genres. It's just a different form of their strategy for recommending songs based on past listening patterns.[32]

Why invest in music recommendation?

Hiring all the engineers to build this recommendation engine is expensive, though — Spotify engineers make hundreds of thousands of dollars a year.[33] So why does Spotify do it?

First, a great recommendation system is a selling point, helping Spotify stand out from rivals like Apple Music. That's because just having a huge music library isn't enough. In business terms, music is a commodity — any song sounds more or less the same whether it's on Spotify or Apple Music or anything else — and anyone with enough money can get the licenses to build a giant library.[34]

So, if all the music streaming services can have effectively the same selection of music, Spotify needs something to differentiate itself from competitors. And Spotify's recommendation system certainly fits the bill — it's widely considered better than Apple Music's.[35]

And since collaborative filtering gets better with more users, Spotify (which already has tons of users) can continue furthering its lead.

The second reason is that personalized recommendations make users more likely to stick with the service.[36] The more you use Spotify, the more the algorithms know about your tastes, and hence the better they can recommend music to you. So if you use Spotify a lot, your recommendations would be pretty good, and you'd lose a lot by jumping to Apple Music, which doesn't know you at all. So this high "switching cost" makes you less likely to jump. (More generally, any personal data you put into an app — like making Spotify playlists — raises the switching cost, since you'd have to recreate that data in any new app you jumped to.[37])

In short, personalized playlists are great for listeners and a savvy business move for Spotify — no wonder more and more apps are offering personalized recommendations.

How does Facebook decide what shows up in your news feed?

Over a billion people look at their Facebook news feed every day, and Americans spend almost as much time on Facebook as they do interacting face-to-face with other people.[38] Because it draws so many eyeballs, the news feed has tremendous power. The news feed can influence our mood, put us in an ideological echo chambers,[39] or even influence who we're going to vote for.[40] In short, what appears in your news feed matters. So how does Facebook decide what to show in your news feed?

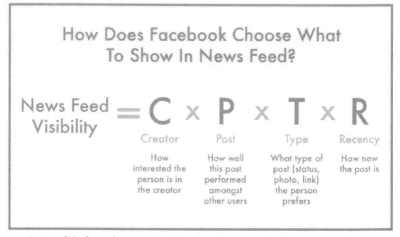

A simplified explanation of Facebook's news feed algorithm. Source: TechCrunch[41]

More specifically, how does Facebook take the hundreds (or thousands) of updates you get every day and sort them for you? Like Google, it uses an algorithm to figure out what's most important. There are about 100,000 personalized factors, but we'll focus on four key ones.[42]

The first factor is who posted it. Facebook will show you more posts from people you've interacted with more (e.g. people you've messaged more or tagged more), with the assumption that you're more likely to engage with their future posts.[43]

Second is the post's quality. The more people have engaged (e.g. liked or commented) with a post, the more interesting Facebook thinks it is, so the more likely it is to appear at the top of your news feed.[44]

Third, the type of post. Facebook figures out what kinds of posts (videos, articles, photos, etc.) you interact with a lot and shows you more of those.[45]

The fourth major factor is "recency": newer stories get ranked higher.[46]

There are plenty more factors, though. TIME found a few:

> Use a phone with a slow mobile connection and you may see less video. Writing 'congratulations' in a comment signals the post is probably about a big life event, so it will get a boost. Liking an article after you clicked it is a stronger positive signal than liking before, since it means you probably read the piece and enjoyed it.[47]

As you can tell, Facebook really tries to maximize the probability that you're going to like or comment on the posts in your news feed, a metric called engagement. After all, the more you like your news feed, the more you're going to scroll down, and the more you scroll down, the more ads you'll see. Ads, of course, are how Facebook makes most of its money.[48]

Score 1.4	Score 1.3	Score 0.8
Photo	Video	Link
Friend	Family	Publisher
100 likes	20 likes	5 likes
8 comments	2 comments	0 comments

An example of how Facebook ranks posts and determines what appears on your news feed. Source: TechCrunch[49]

This algorithm also trains users to act in ways that help Facebook. Everyone wants their posts to show up atop their friends' news feeds, and since Facebook boosts viral posts, people are incentivized to make posts that get shared a lot.[50] More sharing on Facebook leads to more posts, which means Facebook can slot in more ads.

Fighting fake news

Algorithms like Facebook's news feed algorithm are incredibly powerful, but the danger is that they're still easy for crafty hackers to game. With no human oversight, the algorithms could be turned against us.

A famous example is the fake news epidemic that swept Facebook during the 2016 American presidential election.[51]

Recall that the news feed algorithm doesn't consider how true or reputable a post is; it only cares about maximizing engagement.[52] Fake newsmongers took advantage of this to attack politicians they didn't like, posting outrageous and demonstrably false news articles around Facebook. These articles naturally drew many clicks and comments, so Facebook's news feed algorithm propelled them to the top of many people's news feeds.[53]

To Facebook's credit, it's since rolled out updates to its news feed algorithm to try to limit the spread of fake news. In 2018, Facebook announced it would change its algorithm to focus on "meaningful social interactions," meaning it would promote updates from your friends instead of just feeding you news stories. As Facebook admitted, though, measuring "meaningful social interactions" is far harder than just measuring likes and clicks on articles.[54]

Facebook has also been turning to humans to address the flaws in its news feed algorithm. (Ironic, since algorithms are designed to reduce the amount of work humans have to do in the first place, but it acknowledges that algorithms aren't perfect.) For instance, Facebook has introduced features that let people flag fake news posts,[55] and it's started hiring focus groups that scroll through their news feeds and give feedback to the people who design the news feed algorithm.[56] (That's right, you *can* get paid to browse Facebook.)

Algorithms aren't magic spells that run the world. They're just sets of rules (though complex ones) that other people wrote to make computers do a particular task. And, as Facebook shows, sometimes machines and people need to work together.

What technologies do Uber, Yelp, and Pokémon Go have in common?

Suppose you wanted to make your own version of Google Maps. You'd have to track every road, building, city, and shoreline on the planet. You might even need a fleet of cars to drive around the world and take pictures and measurements, as Google has done for Google Maps.[57] And you'd also need to build in panning, zooming, and algorithms to find driving directions between two points.

That is, to put it mildly, very difficult. Even Apple Maps has been criticized for not reaching Google Maps' standard of quality.[58]

So when apps like Uber, Pokémon Go, and Yelp need to include a map to show where available cars are, help players, find wild Pokémon, or display nearby restaurants, they probably do not want to spend billions of dollars and thousands of hours building their own maps.

If you've ever used these apps, you can probably figure out what they do instead: they embed a Google Map in their app. Searching up restaurants? Yelp drops pins on a Google Map centered on your location. Want to Uber downtown? The app draws the route you'll take on a Google Map and calculates the approximate time it'll take to get there.[59]

Google lets you include a small snippet of code in your app to draw a Google Map. It also provides other snippets of code to let you draw on the maps, calculate driving directions between points on the map, and even find out the speed limit for a particular road. All these tools are cheap or even free.[60] These tools are big win for developers; they can use the technology that has taken Google years to perfect with just a small amount of code. There's no need to reinvent the wheel!

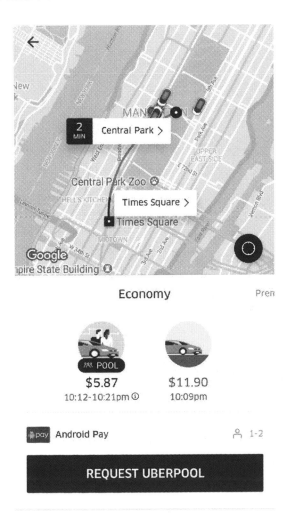

Uber uses the Google Maps API to draw a map of your area and predict your car's travel time. Source: Uber on Android

These snippets of code that let you borrow another app's functionality or data are called APIs, or application programming interfaces. In short, APIs let apps talk to each other. Let's look at three main kinds of APIs.

Three kinds of APIs

The first kind of API, which we'll call "feature APIs," lets one app ask another specialized app to solve a particular problem, like calculating driving directions, sending text messages, or translating sentences. It's like how you could call a plumber or carpenter to fix problems around your house instead of trying to do it yourself. Apps use all kinds of feature APIs. It's a pain to write code that sends emails or text messages, so when apps like Venmo need to send confirmation emails or texts, they'll just use a specialized API.[61] Processing credit card payments is pretty difficult, so Uber outsources this to PayPal's Braintree API,[62] which lets anyone use PayPal's credit card-processing algorithm with just a few lines of code.[63]

The second type of API, which we'll call "data APIs," lets one app ask another app to hand over some interesting information, such as sports scores, recent Tweets, or today's weather. It's like calling the front desk at a hotel to learn which museums and restaurants they recommend. ESPN offers an API that lets you get rosters for every major-league sports team and scores for every game.[64] New York's subway system lets you track where trains are and predict when the next train will arrive at a station.[65] There's even an API to get random images of cats.[66]

The final kind of API, "hardware APIs," lets developers access features of the device itself. Instagram taps into your phone's

Camera API to zoom, focus, and snap photos. Google Maps itself uses your phone's Geolocation API to figure out where in the world you are. Your phone even has sensors called accelerometers and gyroscopes, which fitness apps use to determine which direction you're walking and how fast you're moving.[67]

It's worth noting that APIs aren't perfect. Using an API makes app developers' lives easier, but it also makes their apps dependent on the API.[68] If an email-sending API went down, every app that used it would be unable to send emails. And if Google decided to launch its own ridesharing service, it could — in theory — restrict Uber's access to the Google Maps API to weaken the competition. If Uber built its own mapping service, it wouldn't be at Google's mercy.

Despite the potential business risks, using a specialized company's API is easier, more reliable, and often cheaper than trying to build it yourself.

All this brings us back to the question: what technologies do Uber, Yelp, and Pokémon Go have in common? They all use APIs, namely the Google Maps API, to avoid reinventing the wheel. Indeed, APIs are a core part of pretty much every app out there.

Why does Tinder make you log in with Facebook?

Swipe Right to anonymously
like someone or Swipe Left to
pass

LOG IN WITH FACEBOOK

We don't post anything to Facebook. ∨
By signing in, you agree with our Terms of Service and
Privacy Policy

Tinder on Android. Note that you have to log in with Facebook.

If you've ever used the dating app Tinder, you'll notice that you can log in with your Facebook account before setting up a profile. Once you connect your Facebook profile, Tinder imports information like your profile picture, your age, your list of friends, and the Facebook pages you like.[69] As you might have guessed, this is done through an API that Facebook offers. With this single sign-on (SSO) API, any app can let users create accounts by linking their Facebook profiles.[70]

Why does Tinder use this API? For one, it ensures that there are no empty profiles (which no one would want to swipe on) since some basic information always gets imported from Facebook.[71] Second, requiring Facebook login helps them stop bots and fake accounts, since Facebook already does a lot of work to shut these down.[72] Third, this helps Tinder make better matches: by gathering your friend list, Tinder can show you how many mutual friends you have with each potential match, and that sense of connection probably encourages people to swipe more. Finally, by getting the Facebook profiles of all their users, Tinder can get some deep insights into their user base, such as how old they are, where they live, or what they're interested in.[73] These insights can help Tinder tweak its app's design or advertising strategies.

Signing up with Facebook is also helpful for users. Making your profile with Tinder becomes much faster when most of your basic information and pictures are already imported from Facebook.[74] Seeing more completed profiles and fewer bots improves your experience, as well.[75] And signing up with Facebook means you don't have to remember yet another username and password.[76]

Why would Facebook publish the API that lets people sign in to other websites using their Facebook credentials? Well, when you use Facebook' single sign-on (SSO) API to register for Tinder, Facebook realizes that you're a Tinder user. Facebook gets similar data points when you use Facebook to log into other websites. Facebook can then use this data to target ads at you more effectively, for instance by showing more dating-related ads to Tinder users.[77]

Swiping left on Facebook?

In 2018, Tinder announced that it would let users sign up with their phone number instead of their Facebook account, if they chose.[78] Why?

In a word, competition. In 2018 Facebook announced a new dating service, widely seen as a competitor to Tinder, and Tinder's parent company saw its stock price tumble 20% overnight.[79] Tinder was probably afraid Facebook would cut off its API access and wanted to start building a new way to sign on without being beholden to Facebook.

As this story shows, publishing APIs is a great way for companies to gain data and usage, and using APIs helps apps save development time and offer better features — but it isn't without risk.

Why does every Washington Post article have two versions of every headline?

Take a look at the following two screenshots of the same Washington Post piece. Notice anything?

Notice a difference? The Washington Post shows people different versions of every headline. Source: The Washington Post[80]

The headlines are slightly different! In 2016, the Washington Post rolled out a feature that lets article writers specify two different headlines for every article.[81] But why?

It's actually an experiment that the newspaper runs to maximize the number of clicks on its articles.[82] This experiment automatically shows one version of the headline to one group of visitors; let's say one-half of them, randomly chosen. It shows the other version to the remaining visitors. After letting the experiment run for a while, developers look at particular statistics, or metrics, like the number of clicks on the headline. Developers decide which version is better and show the winning version to everyone. This is a simple but powerful way to improve an app's metrics. For instance, the first version of the above headline was clicked 3.3% of the time, while the bottom version was clicked 3.9%[83] — that's an 18% jump, just by changing a few words!

This technique is called A/B testing. It's a powerful, data-driven way to improve online products.[84] It's named "A/B testing" because you compare at least two versions of a feature, A and B.

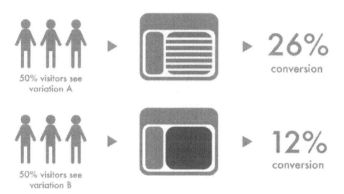

A/B testing shows at least two variations of the same feature (A and B) and compares relevant metrics to decide which variation to push to all users. In this case, everyone would start seeing variation A, which was better at getting users to take a desired action (or "conversion"). Source: VWO[85]

Not sure which marketing catchphrase will get people to buy? Instead of endless debating, just run an A/B test! Not sure if a red or green "sign up" button will get more people to click? Run a test! (If you're curious, the red button got 34% more clicks in one experiment.[86]) Not sure which Tinder profile picture will get you the most swipes? Tinder even lets you run

A/B tests to figure out which of your photos, when shown as your main profile picture, gets you the most right swipes.[87]

All the news that's fit to test

That brings us back to the question: why does every Washington Post article have two versions of each headline? It's part of the Washington Post's A/B testing framework, called Bandito. Bandito tries out different versions of the headline to see which one people click on more, and then shows the winning headline more often.[88]

A/B testing is very popular among news outlets. BuzzFeed uses A/B tests to find the most clickbaity headlines as well.[89] A BuzzFeed competitor called Upworthy actually tries up to 25 versions of the same headline in its quest to find the perfect one.[90] A/B testing is very important: according to Upworthy, the difference between a decent headline and a perfected one is 1,000 vs. 1,000,000 views.[91]

Many more apps and websites use A/B testing. Facebook, for instance, is always rolling out new features to "limited test audiences."[92] Snapchat lets advertisers A/B test their ads to pick the ones that get tapped the most.[93] Even brick-and-mortar stores can do A/B testing: one startup lets stores vary the background music they play to maximize shoppers' spending.[94]

Significance testing

There's one important caveat to keep in mind whenever you're doing statistical tests: you need to check whether your observed findings happened because of something meaningful or were just due to chance. For instance, if you flip a coin six times and get five heads, you can't be confident that the coin is unfairly weighted toward heads — it could just be dumb luck. But if you flipped the coin six hundred times and got five hundred heads, you might be on to something.

When companies perform A/B tests, experimenters report how one version changed a particular metric compared to the other version. They also report a statistic called a p-value, which shows the probability that the difference they observed was due to chance.[95] Usually, if $p < 0.05$ (i.e. there's a less than 5% chance that the difference was just random), they can assume the change was meaningful, or "statistically significant."[96] Otherwise, they can't be sure that their results weren't just dumb luck.

For example, say Amazon made the "Add to Cart" buttons a bit bigger for half their users and found a 2% increase in sales, with $p = 0.15$. While the bigger button seems like a great move, there's a 15% chance that the sales boost was caused by dumb luck, not the button. That 0.15 is greater than 0.05, so Amazon's testers won't roll out the bigger button.

So if you ever get clickbaited by a headline like "18 Food Arguments So Strong That They End Friendships,"[97] don't feel bad — you're up against a powerful blend of social science, software development, and statistics. Like it or not, A/B testing is extremely effective.

Chapter 2.
Operating Systems

Android or iOS? Mac or Windows? Everyone has their own favorite operating systems, or OSes. OSes are the beating heart every computing device, from smartwatches to supercomputers — without them, you couldn't run a single app. Let's see how they work.

Why did BlackBerry fail?

In 2000, BlackBerry launched the world's first smartphone.[1] The phone rose to fame because it let users access the internet and email anywhere, which was great for the always-on world of business.[2] Its QWERTY keyboard made typing far faster than before.[3] People were hopelessly addicted to their so-called "CrackBerries."[4]

By 2009, BlackBerry was a dominant player in the mobile phone space, with 20% market share, more than iOS (14%) and Android (4%) combined.[5] It was so popular that President Barack Obama chose the BlackBerry as his smartphone when he took office in 2009.[6]

But fast forward to the last quarter of 2016, when BlackBerry's market share fell below 0.05%, with the company shipping just over 200,000 phones.[7] Meanwhile, during the same quarter, Android shipped over 350 million units, and iOS shipped 77 million.[8]

Where did BlackBerry go wrong? Let's take a look.

The rise of the iPhone

When Steve Jobs launched the iPhone in 2007,[9] BlackBerry executives didn't take it seriously. They saw it as a flashy toy aimed at young people[10] and not something that competed for BlackBerry's market, which was overwhelmingly comprised of business users.[11]

What BlackBerry failed to realize, though, is that people really enjoyed using their iPhones, with their bright colors and touchscreens.[12] And instead of selling phones to corporate IT managers, as BlackBerry did, Apple sold iPhones directly to consumers — that is, average people like you or us.[13]

The result? With greater access to iPhones, people started carrying two phones: BlackBerries for work but iPhones for personal use.[14] Soon, businesses realized they could save money and keep employees happier by just letting employees use their personal phones for work purposes.[15] Slowly but surely, iPhones started creeping into BlackBerry's treasured enterprise market — a perfect example of the trend known as "consumerization of the enterprise."[16] BlackBerry realized that for smartphones, everyday users, not businesspeople, called the shots.[17]

By the time BlackBerry realized it had to reach consumers directly, it had already fallen behind.[18] To compete with the iPhone, BlackBerry designed a touchscreen phone called the Storm in 2008. But, in their hurry, BlackBerry released the phone before it was ready, and consumers gave the phone negative reviews.[19] Even the BlackBerry CEO admitted it was a flop.[20]

The other main trend that BlackBerry missed was the rise of the "app economy," which we'll cover more in Chapter 4. BlackBerry didn't realize that consumers wanted to do more than just send emails on their phones: they wanted apps, games, and instant messaging.[21] BlackBerry didn't do enough to encourage developers to build apps for their platform. Instead, Apple's App Store grew to have far more apps than BlackBerry's store, which sent customers stampeding toward iPhones.[22]

In short, BlackBerry got complacent, focusing too much on their current users without thinking about growing their new user base.[23] They didn't notice the emerging trends in the software industry. BlackBerry continued to see its phones as business productivity tools, whereas Apple (and Google) rethought phones as versatile "entertainment hubs" for everyday people.[24] Apple read consumers correctly, and they won.[25]

The Hail Mary pass

By 2012, BlackBerry's market share had tumbled from 20% in 2007 to just 7%.[26] That year, BlackBerry appointed a new CEO to try to turn things around.[27] They even launched a new series of high-end phones, the Q10 and Z10, in what a New York Times critic called "BlackBerry's Hail Mary pass."[28]

Unfortunately, the pass fell incomplete.

As BlackBerry sank into third place behind iPhone and Android, it got stuck in a vicious cycle called the "chicken-and-egg problem."[29] Developers wouldn't build apps for the BlackBerry platform if it didn't have any users, and users wouldn't buy BlackBerries unless there were enough apps.[30] Imagine if no one would walk into a party unless there were already enough people there — nobody would ever come in.[31] BlackBerry tried hard to entice developers to their platform, even offering $10,000 to anyone who made a BlackBerry app in 2012.[32] But it still didn't work.

BlackBerry continued its downward spiral — and the rest, as they say, is history.

Why does Google make Android free to phone manufacturers?

Google's Android mobile operating system is free for both consumers and phone manufacturers. The likes of Samsung and LG can slap Android on their phones without paying Google anything.[33] But Android now rakes in over $31 billion a year in revenue for Google.[34] How on earth could a free product earn Google so much money?

Google's strategy begins with getting as many people as possible to use Android.[35] Clearly, making Android free is working: Android powers over 80% of the world's smartphones.[36]

With such a high market share, Google can use a variety of tactics to earn money off Android.

First off, Google forces any phone manufacturer that uses Android to install all the core Google apps, like YouTube and Google Maps, by default. In the US, Google even forces phone manufacturers to put the Google search bar no more than one swipe away from the home screen.[37] By getting more people on its apps, Google can get more data, show more ads, and thus make more money.[38]

A second source of income — which is smaller but still considerable — is app purchases.[39] In most countries, Google insists that phone manufacturers prominently feature Google Play, Android's app store, on the home screen of any Android phone.[40] This is designed to drive more users to download apps from the Google Play marketplace. And whenever someone buys an app or makes an in-app purchase, Google takes a 30% cut.[41] Each purchase nets Google a small amount of money, but it adds up: Google earns $25 billion a year from these commissions.[42] More Google Play users leads to more downloads, which leads to more commission revenue.

Third, making Android more prevalent could help Google keep more ad revenue for itself.[43] Whenever an iOS user clicks on ads in Google Search, Apple keeps a sizable chunk of the ad revenue that would otherwise go to Google.[44] Plus, Google pays Apple an estimated $12 billion per year just to make Google Search the default search engine on iOS.[45] So you can see why Google would prefer if people ran Google searches on Androids instead of iPhones.

More Android users equals more money for Google, so it's no surprise Google is giving away Android for free.

Why open-source?

Android isn't just free — it's also open-source,[46] meaning that anyone can make and distribute their own spin-offs of Android.[47] There's a vibrant community of developers making custom "flavors" of Android, like the popular LineageOS (formerly known as CyanogenMod).[48] You can replace your phone's Android operating system with LineageOS to get improved speed, customization, and features.[49]

A phone running the Android spin-off LineageOS, demonstrating a custom feature for developers that can't be found on normal Android. Source: Aral Balkan[50]

Android is literally open-source to the core; it's built around the "kernel" of the open-source operating system Linux, which is also used in some of the world's biggest supercomputers.[51] The kernel is a bit of software that lets apps talk to the device's hardware, like by reading and writing files, connecting to the keyboard and Wi-Fi, and so on.[52] A kernel is like a car's engine: the computer literally wouldn't run without a kernel.

So why did Google make Android open-source? The first reason is for ease of engineering. Using Linux's pre-built, open-source kernel saves Android developers a lot of work,[53] since the Linux developers have been constantly improving their kernel since 1991.[54] And Linux works on an incredible range of devices, from supercomputers to video game consoles,[55] so by adopting Linux, Android automatically became able to run on a vast variety of hardware.

Second, because Android is open source, phone manufacturers get to customize the interface, which helps their phones stand out.[56] That's a good incentive for phone makers to pick Android over another operating system.

And third, making Android open-source brings more people into the Android and Google ecosystem.[57] Since Android is open-source, people who want to massively customize their phones are much more likely to use a spin-off of Android than iOS, which isn't open source and hence can't be customized as easily. The spin-offs are fine by Google. Even if someone uses an Android spin-off rather than the standard version of Android, they're probably still doing Google searches and using Google apps. Since more users equals more money, promoting open-source actually helps Google's bottom line.[58]

To summarize, why did Google make Android free to phone manufacturers? While it might not directly make Google any money, this move helps Android get more users, more app purchases, and more searches on Android — all of which helps Google haul in profits.

Why do Android phones come pre-installed with so many junk apps?

Ever bought an Android phone? When you unwrap it, you realize pretty quickly that it's crammed with all kinds of useless apps you never asked for: NFL Mobile, Candy Crush, Samsung Pay, Verizon Navigator (a Google Maps knockoff that costs $5 a month), you name it.[59] Smartphone makers like Samsung, mobile carriers like Verizon, and phone sellers euphemistically call these "pre-installed apps" and claim that they showcase the functionality and performance of the phone.[60] But most of us just call it "bloatware," and nobody likes it.[61]

Most pre-installed apps can't be uninstalled and, by default, run constantly in the background, which eats up battery, makes your phone run slower, and wastes storage space.[62] One reviewer found that his new Samsung Galaxy phone had 37 bloatware apps that ate up 12GB of his 64GB of storage as soon as he opened the box.[63] Sometimes things get truly absurd, like when Verizon once pre-installed a bloatware app on Galaxy S7s that would download *other* bloatware apps without the user knowing.[64]

*An Android phone full of bloatware. It appears that the bloatware apps
were so annoying that the phone's owner put the apps into their own
folder just to get them out of the way!*

It's not that easy to fight back, either. While you can disable
some bloatware apps and prevent them from running in the
background and wasting your battery, they'll still take up
storage on your phone.[65]

The business of bloat

So why does your phone come with so much junk? Mobile carriers and smartphone manufacturers aren't just trying to be cruel. Bloatware is at the center of a lucrative business model.

The bloatware business model arose when smartphone manufacturers like Samsung and mobile carriers like AT&T realized that the American market for smartphones and data plans is pretty much saturated. That is, almost everyone who wants a phone and data plan already has one, so manufacturers and carriers can't grow their revenue much by just selling phones and data plans. Instead, they've turned to new ways of making money — which leads them straight to bloatware.[66] There are two big ways carriers and phone makers make money off bloatware.

First, app makers can pay carriers and phone makers to pre-install their apps. For instance, Verizon once offered to pre-install big companies' apps for $1 to $2 per installation.[67] In other words, if your Verizon phone has 10 bloatware apps, Verizon could have made an easy $20 off you. It's free money for carriers and phone makers, and it helps app makers get their apps in front of people — which is important, since the majority of Americans download exactly zero apps a month.[68] The only loser, of course, is the consumer.

Second, carriers and phone makers also pre-install their own apps, which are often expensive knockoffs of popular free apps. For instance, Samsung pre-installs its own Android app store, and AT&T pre-installs its own Navigator, a $10-a-month clone of Google Maps.[69] Verizon's Message+ is like Facebook Messenger but charges you for texts you send over Wi-Fi.[70]

Why do carriers and phone makers pre-install these apps? Again, it's easy money: Samsung earns a commission from paid apps and themes from its app store,[71] and carriers and phone makers make money from the pricey knockoff apps. These companies hope that users won't notice that there are free alternatives to the bloatware apps and, instead, will use (and pay for!) the default pre-installed apps. Defaults are powerful: Apple made Apple Maps the default navigation app on iPhones, and even though most customers preferred Google Maps, Apple Maps became more popular than Google Maps on iPhones by 2015 — thanks to Apple Maps' position as the default.[72]

However, many users seem to be rebelling against bloatware. For one, many don't use this useless software. Even though Samsung's bloatware chat app, ChatOn, has 100 million users, they only use it for an average of 6 seconds a month,[73] compared to Facebook's 20 hours a month.[74] And second, customers have started giving many bloatware apps low reviews in app stores.[75] The danger of all this? Frustrated users could just abandon the bloated phones altogether, which would make the bloatware strategy backfire.[76] But are there non-bloated alternative phones?

Bloat-free iPhones

If you have an iPhone, here's a reason to smile: iPhones don't have bloatware.[77] But why?

Think first about how Apple makes money: most of their revenue comes from selling hardware[78] — over 60% of Apple's income comes from iPhone sales alone.[79] Plus, Apple's brand, driven by the smooth and refined experience of using their products, is one of Apple's core strengths.[80] So bloatware wouldn't align with Apple's money-making strategy, and it would also weaken their treasured user experience.

Why can't carriers just slide in their own bloatware? For starters, Apple outright forbids carriers like Sprint or AT&T from putting bloatware on iPhones.[81] That might seem to make Android more attractive for carriers. But because so many customers demand iPhones, it would be foolish for carriers to refuse to support iPhones — and so they're forced to go along with Apple's bloatware ban.[82]

But how about those Apple apps that come pre-installed on iPhones, like Safari, iCloud, and Apple Maps? Some users don't like them: when Apple rolled out Apple Maps in 2012, customers said it "sucked" and was "the phone's biggest drawback."[83] We wouldn't call these apps bloatware, though, because you can now delete almost all of Apple's pre-installed apps. The few that you can't uninstall, like Messages and Camera, are core to the operating system,[84] so it's understandable why you can't get rid of them.

Non-bloated Androids

Finally, there's a silver lining to this story: some Android phones are getting rid of bloatware.

When Google's flagship Pixel phone launched in 2016, Google announced it wouldn't inject any of its own bloatware in a bid to have a user experience as polished as the iPhone's.[85] However, carriers could still inject some bloatware; Verizon, for instance, stuffed apps like My Verizon and VZ Messages into the first-edition Pixel.[86]

But whether through technical limitations or strict policies, Google managed to ban carrier bloatware over the next few years, and when the Pixel 3 came out in 2018, it was free of all bloatware.[87]

What is the world's third-biggest mobile OS?

If you had to name the world's three biggest mobile operating systems, you'd definitely name Android and iOS. But what's the third-biggest? It's not BlackBerry — that operating system is dead.[88] And it's not Windows Phone, which is dead too.[89]

The answer is KaiOS, a lightweight OS for internet-connected feature phones. It's specifically targeted at India, where it's become the country's second-most-popular mobile OS.[90]

Competing against the twin titans of mobile is extremely difficult, and even a giant like Microsoft couldn't do it.[91] Yet KaiOS powers 15% of the phones in India, far behind Android's 70% but more than iOS's 10%.[92] So what is KaiOS, and how did it grow to third place when so many other mobile operating systems failed?

KaiOS lets internet-connected feature phones run many popular apps.
Source: DeCode[93]

The Jio Phone

The story of KaiOS begins with Jio, an Indian telecom provider started in 2016 as a subsidiary of the telecom giant Reliance. Jio was revolutionary, offering free voice calls forever and 1 GB of mobile data for just 50 rupees (then about $0.75) — gargantuan discounts compared to the existing Indian telecom providers. (In fact, at the time Jio offered data for one-tenth the price of the average American carrier!)[94] Jio was an instant hit, gaining 100 million subscribers within six months.[95]

But Jio realized that 500 million Indians didn't have smartphones, which were often out of their price range, and that this was limiting Jio's growth. So in 2017 Jio announced the Jio Phone, a lightweight feature phone that was effectively free — you'd pay a 1500 rupee (then $20) deposit but get it back after 3 years.[96]

The Jio Phone managed to offer reliable 4G cheaply by axing the touchscreen, shrinking the screen resolution, and offering just a bare-bones camera. It even supported 25 languages. Suddenly, farmers in rural India were able to use apps and stream video where before they barely knew what phones were.[97] Indeed, India mostly skipped the desktop phase and jumped straight to mobile,[98] so the Jio Phone was many Indians' first taste of modern tech.

The Jio Phone, a $20 phone that runs KaiOS. It packs cheap data and free calls. Source: GadgetsNow[99]

The Jio Phone needed an operating system, but Android — even Android's lightweight Go variant — demanded smartphone specs and features like a touchscreen.[100] So Jio turned to an upstart operating system called KaiOS, designed to offer an app-based, internet-powered experience for feature phones.[101] KaiOS would be pre-installed on all Jio Phones.[102]

Rising from the ashes

KaiOS was built atop Firefox OS, a previous attempt to create a mobile OS for developing countries. Mozilla, the creator of the Firefox browser and then Firefox OS, realized that Android and iOS apps are too bulky for lightweight phones and had to be downloaded, while websites are lightweight and load instantly. So Mozilla made Firefox OS a web-based operating system. There were "apps" for YouTube, Gmail, calculators, and such, but they were just custom-built websites, also known as HTML5 apps.[103]

Firefox OS's problem, though, was that it was designed for smartphones with touchscreens — which meant it was going head-to-head with Android. And as Android started offering cheaper and cheaper smartphones for developing markets, it crowded Firefox OS out of its niche.[104] Firefox OS never got traction and shut down in 2016.[105]

KaiOS realized that, while Firefox OS's business strategy was flawed, its technical underpinnings were sound. Since Firefox OS was open source, KaiOS picked up the old code and created a new operating system that was still web-based but now worked for touchscreen-less feature phones. And instead of trying to fight for Android's slice of the pie, KaiOS was expanding the pie, going for the market — feature phones — that Android would never get into.[106] (While low-end Androids might be cheap, they still can't match the Jio Phone.)

KaiOS's second smart move was realizing that the people demanded apps like WhatsApp and YouTube. So it partnered with Google to create custom-built versions of apps like Google Search, Google Maps, YouTube, and the Google Assistant for KaiOS — these apps were presumably had a better user experience than just loading the mobile website.[107]

The Jio Phone grew like crazy, selling 40 million units in its first year and a half on the market.[108] And KaiOS has done great too, with over 85 million phones sold in over 100 countries.[109]

Can Macs get viruses?

For years, one of the biggest selling points of Macs was that they "don't get viruses."[110] In 2006, as part of Apple's famous "Get a Mac" advertising campaign, Apple even made an ad that showed the healthy "Mac" character giving a tissue to the sickly "PC" character.[111]

But are Macs really immune?

First things first: Macs can't get Windows viruses.[112] That's just because any app made for Windows, whether it's a Google Chrome installer or the nastiest virus out there, won't run on a Mac. The platforms are just incompatible.

Though Windows viruses won't affect Macs, viruses built specifically for Macs can definitely infect them.[113] But many people are adamant that Macs don't get viruses.[114] How could that be?

Macs' strengths

People who say that Macs are invincible have two main lines of argument. One argument is that Macs are so uncommon that hackers don't bother targeting them, and another is that Macs are so secure that a virus wouldn't be able to infect them anyway.[115]

Let's look at the first argument. It's true that Macs are uncommon: as of 2017, just one in 25 computers worldwide is a Mac, while most of the rest are Windows PCs.[116] And since hackers usually just want to make money, the theory is that they'd focus on Windows, which gives them more targets.[117]

That's not a bad argument, but there's a small catch: hacking a Mac might earn a hacker more money than hacking a PC. Macs are more common in wealthier countries, often clocking in at 20-30% of the computer market share in western nations, and Mac owners tend to be much wealthier than their Windows-toting friends.[118] That might give hackers more of a reason to target Mac owners, since Mac-owning victims would be more likely to fork over more money. So the argument that "Macs are too uncommon" is legitimate, though flawed.

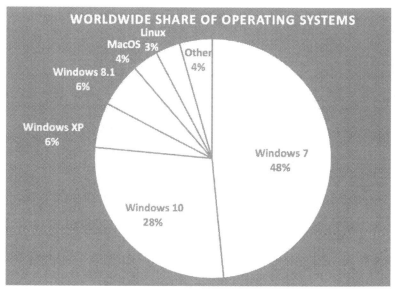

The worldwide market share of desktop operating systems. Notice that Macs are just 4% of all computers, while Windows PCs are over 88%! Source: NetMarketShare[119]

How about the claim that Macs are more secure than PCs? Macs do have some built-in security features that make them harder to hack. By default, Mac users can't run potentially-risky software or change certain setting unless they enter their password, while Windows is less strict.[120] That means that, on a Mac, rogue software can't do as many damaging things without the user noticing. Macs also have a feature called "sandboxing," where a virus in one part of the computer can't easily spread to others.[121] It's like if you locked the door to every room in a house individually: even if a burglar broke into one room, they couldn't get to other rooms without extra effort. And finally, macOS has built-in malware scanners and blocks apps whose authors weren't approved by Apple.[122] Put these together, and hacking a Mac looks more challenging than hacking a PC.

Macs' vulnerabilities

But despite Macs' security features, they can — and do — get viruses. For instance, in 2012, over 600,000 Macs were infected by a virus called Flashback, the biggest Mac epidemic to date.[123] Over the next few years, several more Mac viruses, including ones called Rootpipe and KitM.A, started appearing.[124]

Clearly, Macs aren't immune to viruses. In fact, one 2017 analysis found that macOS actually had more security flaws than Windows 10.[125]

And no matter how secure your operating system, you're always at risk for "social engineering" attacks like phishing, which trick people into giving away personal information that hackers can use to defraud them.[126]

Chapter 3.
App Economics

In 2010, Apple trademarked the catchphrase "there's an app for that."[1] And, indeed, apps seem to have taken over the world. Multi-billion-dollar companies like Uber (founded 2008[2]), Airbnb (also 2008[3]), and Snapchat (2011[4]) are based on little more than an app. This entire "app economy" is estimated to be worth $100 billion.[5]

So how do those little icons on your phone screen lead to billions of dollars in economic activity? The rules for this "app economy" are very different than the rules of the "traditional" economy, where you walk into a store and buy items off the shelf. Let's explore this strange new world.

Why is almost every app free to download?

A medium pizza might cost you $9.99. A car wash will set you back $15. You'll need to fork over about $45 a month for a data plan.

But almost every app you have on your phone is free. Instagram, Snapchat, Dropbox, Venmo, Google Maps — all free. In fact, of all the highest-grossing apps on Android and iOS, only one paid app cracks the top 100, and it's Minecraft.[6] (Meanwhile, the mobile game Fortnite raked in over a billion dollars in 2018 despite being free to play.[7])

And yet, many companies that produce these free-to-download apps are raking in millions. For instance, the Snapchat app is totally free, yet Snapchat's parent company (Snap, Inc.) was valued at $33 billion when it went public in 2017.[8] It shows just how different the app economy is from the "normal" economy: if Pizza Hut said they were going to make money while giving away pizzas for free, you'd think they were crazy.

So how do app makers make money without selling software? They've come up with some pretty clever business models, also known as "monetization" strategies. Let's take a look at one of the most popular ones, called "freemium."

Freemium: *more features, at a price*

If you've ever played Candy Crush, you'll notice that the app is free, but once you start playing, you're bombarded with offers to use real money to buy extra lives or to unlock new levels.[9] Similarly, Tinder lets you "swipe" on potential romantic partners — but only a few dozen a day. If you want to get more "swipes," you'll need to pay for Tinder Plus, a monthly subscription.[10]

This business model is called "freemium,"[11] and it's pretty simple. Give away your app for free, so tons of people will download it, then make them pay for extra "premium" features (hence the name "freemium").[12] Freemium is everywhere: it's how many mobile games like Candy Crush and Pokémon Go make money,[13] and it's extremely popular among popular apps like Tinder,[14] Spotify,[15] and Dropbox.[16]

Freemium apps usually use one of two strategies to make money: in-app purchases or paid subscriptions. Let's dive into both.

In-app purchases

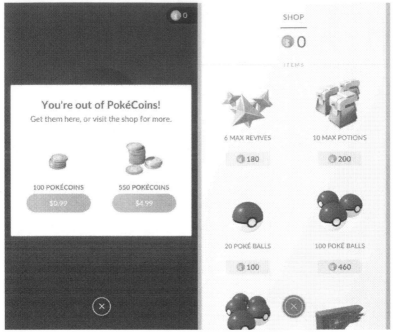

Pokémon Go is free to play, but you can use real money to buy coins, which can be swapped for in-game goodies. Source: Pokémon Go on Android

In-app purchases usually refer to extra features or virtual items in the app that you can pay real money for.[17] In-app purchases are mobile games' bread and butter. Candy Crush, as we mentioned, peddles extra lives. Pokémon Go lets you buy coins, which can be redeemed for extra Poké Balls or Potions that'll let you beef up your pet monsters.[18] Some in-app purchases are just for cosmetic purposes: Fortnite players shell out hundreds of dollars to customize their avatars with things like shirts and dance moves.[19]

Paid upgrades are nothing new for games, though. Even decades-old PC games like *World of Warcraft*[20] or *SimCity*[21] have long offered paid "expansion packs." Console games also offer in-app purchases via downloadable content, or DLC, that let you buy access new items, dungeons, and challenges.[22]

In-app purchases are primarily used in games, though a few standard apps offer them. Snapchat, for instance, lets you buy your own customized geofilters for special events.[23] And many Android/iOS apps that normally show ads will let you buy an upgrade to remove them.[24]

One big reason that game and app creators love in-app purchases are that they're pure profit: once you've built your app or game, it costs basically nothing to give a user virtual items like outfits or geofilters (in other words, the marginal cost is zero).[25] Poorly or dishonestly designed in-app purchases can lead to backlash, though, like when customers grew outraged after free-to-play Facebook games tricked children into paying hundreds of dollars for in-game items.[26]

Paid subscriptions

Besides in-app purchases, the other major "freemium" business model is paid subscriptions, similar to your monthly phone bill. Usually, subscriptions let you unlock useful new features in exchange for a monthly payment. Paid subscriptions are easy to spot; just look for "Plus," "Premium," or "Gold."

Subscriptions are more the territory of non-game apps, and they are everywhere. We mentioned Tinder Plus, which lets you pay a small monthly fee to get unlimited swipes and extra features.[27] LinkedIn requires a monthly payment for LinkedIn Premium, which lets you message people you aren't connected to.[28] You can stream music for free with Spotify, but to remove ads and store music offline, you'll have to pay for the Premium subscription.[29] Even Microsoft, which has for years made money selling Office, now offers some Office apps for free but encourages users to buy annual subscriptions to Office 365.[30]

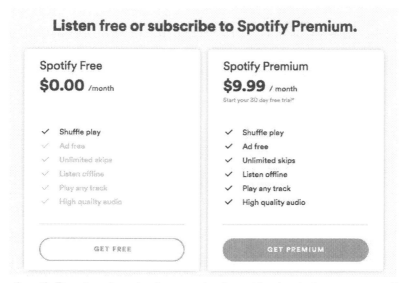

Spotify Premium is a classic example of a paid subscription: pay a small monthly fee to get extra features. Source: Spotify[31]

Some websites and apps have also started using subscriptions: the New York Times, for instance, lets you read a few articles a month for free but makes you pay monthly to get unlimited access.[32]

There are two big reasons app makers are turning to subscriptions. First, they provide a steady and reliable source of income, whereas relying on one-off purchases leads to big spikes in revenue when you release a new update and big crashes at other times. Second, customers who subscribe tend to stick with the app longer (probably because they feel they have a long-term relationship with the app instead of a one-off interaction), meaning they'll pay the company more money throughout their lives. In business terms, customers will have a higher "lifetime value" (LTV), and maximizing LTV is widely seen as the holy grail for digital businesses.[33]

Whale hunting

As you've probably experienced, most people are willing to pay exactly zero dollars for software: one study found that only 6% of all iOS app downloads were for paid apps.[34] Yes, even $1 is too much for most people. But while most people won't pay anything, the small fraction of people who use a certain app the most are often willing to pay a lot of money. Economists call this the 80-20 rule or the Pareto principle: 20% of your customers will generate 80% of your revenue, and 80% of your customers will generate the other 20%.[35]

The key for app developers is to find that 20% of people who want to pay money (called "whales" in the industry, probably because they're rare but huge) and squeeze as much cash as possible out of them.[36] These whales are big: the average paying user of a mobile game spends $86.50 on in-app purchases every year.[37] Some whales are of positively Moby Dickian proportions: in 2015, the mobile title *Game of War: Fire Age* earned almost $550 per paying user.[38]

Because the heaviest users of an app are the most likely to pay, most in-app purchases or subscriptions are aimed at the most dedicated users. For instance, remember how Tinder lets you pay for unlimited swipes. Most users will never swipe enough to run out of the few dozen free swipes you get per day, but the most enthusiastic Tinderers will quickly run out. And because these users are so committed to Tinder, they won't mind paying a few dollars to get more use out of it — whereas most casual users would balk at even a small fee.[39]

In short, the freemium strategy is this: give away the app for free to draw in a massive number of users,[40] find the "power users" who love the app, and charge them — either once or via a recurring subscription — for extra features.

But how can a company make money without even charging its users? Read on.

How does Facebook make billions without charging users a penny?

Freemium can be highly profitable. But think about Google and Facebook. You've probably been using their apps — from Maps and Docs to Instagram and the Facebook app — for years, yet you've likely never paid them a single cent.[41] So if they don't use freemium, how do they make money?

The simple answer: *targeted ads*. Let's break down what both of these words mean.

Ad auctions

As you've probably seen, apps and websites have long used ads to make money. They'll charge advertisers a small fee to show their ads on the app or website. But how exactly do apps and websites know how much to charge for ads? There are two main approaches.

First, apps and websites can charge advertisers a small fee every time someone views an ad, a strategy called Pay-Per-Impression, or PPI..[42] Since so many people view ads, apps and websites usually charge in increments of 1,000 views; that is, the pricing for an ad campaign could be $5 for 1,000 "impressions." Because advertisers often pay per thousand views, Pay-Per-Impression is more often called Cost-Per-Mille, or CPM.[43] (*Mille* comes from the prefix *milli*, as in *millimeter*.)

Alternatively, apps and websites can charge advertisers whenever someone actually clicks an ad, which is called Cost-

Per-Click, or CPC. CPC is less frequently known as PPC, or Pay-Per-Click. [44]

Google[45] and Facebook[46] offer both Cost-Per-Mille (CPM) and Cost-Per-Click (CPC) advertising to earn money from ads. An advertiser who wants to place an ad on Google or Facebook products, like Google Search or Facebook's news feed, specifies their "bid," or how much they'd be willing to pay per click or view. Every time a visitor loads a page, all the advertisers face off in an instant "auction," and the winner's ad gets shown.[47]

Having a higher bid makes your ad more likely to show up, but the highest bidder doesn't necessarily win. Google and Facebook consider a few other criteria, like how relevant the ad is, to decide which app to show. Why? More relevant ads will probably get clicked more, so they might make more money than a less relevant ad with a higher bid. Think about it: if you were Google, would you rather show a $5 ad that gets clicked 10 times or a $2 ad that gets clicked 100 times?[48]

Ads are how Google and Facebook make money, but the reason they make *so much* money is because of a technique called targeting.[49]

Targeting ads

Would you ever click on an ad for sofas unless you were actively shopping for furniture? Probably not. That's one of the pitfalls of ads you might see on TV or in a magazine: blasting your message to everyone can be wasteful when only a small audience would be interested.[50] But what if advertisers strategically showed you sofa ads only when you were moving into a dorm room or new house and needed new furniture? That would probably be more effective.

This "ad targeting" strategy is how Google and Facebook really set themselves apart. Because you do so much on Google's and Facebook's apps and websites, these companies know a lot about what you like. They then use this data to target ads to you, which lets them rake in advertising dollars while giving you the service for free.[51]

For example, if Google notices that you search for "guide for choosing a watch" or "cost of a cheap watch," Google could infer that you're shopping for a wristwatch. Then they could show you ads for watches when you're doing future searches. Since these hyper-targeted ads are more relevant to you, you're more likely to click on them than non-targeted ads.[52] More clicks lead to more purchases, so targeted ads help advertisers make more money.

In other words, targeting ads improves the "click-through rate," or CTR, which gets advertisers more bang for their buck. Since they have more data on users than anyone else, Google and Facebook can target ads extremely well, and so they can charge advertisers top dollar.[53] The business of targeting ads based on user data is lucrative: Google and Facebook rely on ads for almost all of their revenue.[54] Facebook makes over $30 billion a year from ads[55] — which is nearly 99% of its overall revenue.[56]

So, are targeted ads good or evil? Privacy advocates are worried about how these big companies can track your every click[57] and know vast amounts about your interests, habits, and activities.[58]

But maybe that's just the cost of doing business: there's no such thing as a free lunch, and instead of paying for Google and Facebook products with money, you're paying with personal data.[59] This debate is summed up in the Silicon Valley proverb: "if you aren't paying for the product, you *are* the product."[60]

Ad dominion

Targeted ads are powerful, and nobody does them better than Google and Facebook. The two companies have a near chokehold on advertising, together accounting for about half of the entire mobile ad market.[61] It's much harder for smaller startups to make money off targeted ads because advertisers would rather just buy from Google and Facebook, who have far more user data.

The one company that has been able to scare Google and Facebook's ad divisions is Amazon, which has become the US's third-biggest ad platform.[62] Over half of people, when searching for products to buy online, now start their search on Amazon instead of Google.[63] With this increased share of eyeballs, Amazon can now place ads directly in a listing of items for sale, which is a place where people are already highly motivated to buy things. And since Amazon knows exactly what you buy, it probably can figure out what you might want to buy with frightening accuracy.[64]

In other words, Amazon has begun competing with Google for ads that lead directly to a purchase, or "direct-response ads."[65] So it is indeed possible for new players to get into targeted ads, though Amazon isn't exactly a tiny startup anymore.

Selling your data? Not quite.

Finally, it's important to point out that Google and Facebook — and most other software companies that use ads — don't sell your data to advertisers. Advertisers submit ads to Google and Facebook, and the two companies use your data to decide what ads to show you. Your data is used extensively on Google and Facebook computers, but it never leaves them.[66] In fact, it actually helps Google and Facebook to keep user data to themselves, since it forces advertisers to keep coming back to them.[67]

However, Facebook has come under fire in recent years for giving away user data without telling users. It partnered with device makers like Apple and Samsung, handing over user data in exchange for special placement on phones.[68] Facebook also shared user data with Amazon in exchange for Amazon data that would help power Facebook's friend suggestion feature.[69]

In short, ad-driven companies — for the most part — aren't selling your data. As PCWorld put it, it's more accurate to say that they're selling *you*.[70] And this strategy is so successful that it can build billion-dollar companies that charge users nothing. That's the remarkable part of the app economy.

Why do news websites have so much "sponsored content?"

When you think of ads, you might think of banner ads: those flashy, animated rectangles that show up on webpages or at the bottom of apps. They're still popular on websites, although fewer and fewer major apps have banner ads nowadays, probably because ads are annoying and take up valuable space.[71] Plus, people rarely click on banner ads anymore, so they aren't very profitable. In fact, people only intentionally click on banner ads 0.17% of the time[72] — that's roughly 1 out of every 600 ads you see.

But now, there's a new kind of ad on the block, and it's less intrusive and harder to ignore.[73] When you scroll through your Instagram feed, you might notice some posts that aren't from your friends but rather from companies trying to sell you something.[74] Snapchat lets advertisers make filters that millions of users can see,[75] and Twitter even lets advertisers buy hashtags that start "trending."[76]

The word you see attached to all of these? "Sponsored."[77] Sponsored content, also called "native advertising," means ads that blend in with normal content, making viewers more likely to take the ads seriously instead of ignoring them.[78]

Sponsored content is growing especially quickly in the world of journalism.[79] Advertisers can pay to include legitimate-looking articles (which are really just ads) amidst normal material on websites like the New York Times, CNN, NBC, and the Wall Street Journal.[80] Newer media companies like BuzzFeed also love native advertising.[81] An increasing amount of "journalism" is becoming dressed-up advertising. For example, the New York Times once ran a story about why the traditional jail system doesn't work for female inmates. It was a well-researched and engaging story, but it was all an advertisement for the Netflix series *Orange is the New Black.*[82]

A piece in the New York Times about women in prisons. It's a well-written article, but it's also a native ad for the Netflix show "Orange is the New Black." Source: The New York Times[83]

Sponsored content is highly effective for advertisers: native ads are clicked on over twice as much as banner ads.[84] And it's become a powerful revenue stream for news publications. For instance, in 2016, the Atlantic expected to earn three-quarters of its digital ad revenue from native ads.[85] And, since the internet has obliterated journalism's traditional business model, native advertising might be one of the few things keeping newspapers afloat.

Native advertising is powerful, but it's dangerous all the same because it makes it harder for people to distinguish facts from marketing.[86] In fact, Reuters found that 43% of American readers [87]felt "disappointed or deceived" by native advertising.[88] And, more fundamentally, native advertising breaks down the walls that news publications have traditionally placed between journalists and businesspeople.[89] In other words, if the same people who report the news are now writing advertisements, journalistic integrity could be compromised.[90]

Is there a silver lining to native advertising? Maybe. One study found that 22% of consumers thought native advertising was educational, versus just 4% who thought the same of banner ads.[91]

How does Airbnb make money?

Amazon, Uber, and Airbnb are all free to download, never charge you for using the app, and show you few, if any, ads. So how do they make money?

"Marketplace" or "platform" apps like these, which connect buyers to sellers (or riders to drivers, etc.), earn commission by sneaking some fees into the purchases you make.[92] It's like how the government makes money using a sales tax or how a real estate agent charges commission whenever they help you buy or sell a house.

For example, Airbnb includes a "services fee" whenever you make a booking. Hosts pay 3%, and guests pay another 6-12%.[93] These fees provide most of Airbnb's revenue.[94]

Guests

1 guest	⌄

$46 × 2 nights	$92
Cleaning fee ❓	$25
Service fee ❓	$16
Total	**$133**

Book

Airbnb makes money by charging you a small "service fee" on top of any reservation you make. Source: Airbnb[95]

Other marketplace apps also take commissions. Uber grabs 20-25% of the money that drivers earn.[96] Amazon takes a cut when third-party sellers list and sell their items on the platform.[97] The exact cut varies by product, but one that we can tell you from experience is that Amazon takes between 30% and 65% of book revenues.[98]

So that's how most marketplace apps make money. Can any marketplace selling apps make money without charging commission? Read on.

How does the app Robinhood let you trade stocks with zero commission?

Buying and selling stocks is a great way to invest your earnings and make extra money, but with every trade you have to pay some commission to a broker. Or do you? The stock-trading app Robinhood lets you make trades for free.[99] That's right, zero commission.

So how do they stay in business? There are two main ways Robinhood makes money.[100]

First, they employ the classic freemium model to help "power" users get more functionality. Robinhood Gold lets you trade after hours (i.e. for a few hours before and after the normal trading day, which is 9:30am to 4pm EST), and it lets you borrow money from Robinhood to make additional purchases beyond what you can currently afford.[101]

The second way is pretty clever. Robinhood earns interest from unused money sitting in users' accounts in much the same way that you earn interest by stashing your unused money in a bank.[102]

As you can see, apps are getting crafty with their business models. Let's finish the chapter with a look at some even more creative approaches.

How can apps make money without showing ads or charging users?

Every app we've talked about so far makes money by showing ads or charging users (if not up front, then through subscriptions, in-app purchases, or commissions). Is there another way for app businesses to stay afloat? Can apps get money from anyone besides users or advertisers?

As it turns out, the answer is yes. Let's finish up the chapter by looking at some of these clever business models.

First, you could charge people besides users or advertisers. The travel-booking service Wanderu, for instance, helps you find the best bus tickets and refers you to the websites of bus lines like Greyhound and Megabus to purchase them. Wanderu doesn't charge shoppers anything, but it takes a small commission from the bus lines for the privilege of sending customers their way.[103]

Or, apps could try to survive without making any revenue at all. It sounds impossible, but in the world of tech, it can happen — temporarily, at least.

Some apps just live on borrowed time (and venture capitalist money), providing free service until they get large enough that they can start earning — in other words, "grow first, monetize later."[104] For instance, Venmo makes no money from your payments to friends. It charges nothing if you transfer money between bank accounts, and if you're transferring money from your credit card, it only charges you the same fee (3%) that it's required to pay to the payment processing company.[105]

Then, in 2018, Venmo decided it had a big enough user base to start monetizing. It announced that you could now pay for Ubers with Venmo and rolled out a Venmo-based debit card. In both cases, Venmo charges merchants a small fee. Some have also speculated that Venmo could start targeting ads at users since it now knows exactly what they spend money on.[106]

Other apps just hope to be bought before their money runs out. For instance, a free email app called Mailbox hit the market in 2013, and soon it was delivering 60 million messages a day.[107] Then, within a month of launch, Dropbox bought the app and the team behind it[108] for $100 million.[109] There's a slightly tragic ending, though: Dropbox killed the app in 2015 and shuffled the employees to different teams.[110] Call us cynical, but Mailbox's ability to grow explosively and get to an attractive "exit" was because it offered its service for free.[111]

In short, app makers have had to become ever craftier now that users demand free-to-download apps. The remarkable part is that app makers never seem to run out of clever ways to monetize. What's the next big monetization strategy? Now that you've read this chapter, maybe you'll be able to figure it out.

Chapter 4.
The Internet

In 2006, Alaska Senator Ted Stevens, tasked with creating new internet regulations, made this infamous speech in which he tried to explain how the internet worked:

> Ten movies streaming across that, that Internet, and what happens to your own personal Internet? I just the other day got... an Internet was sent by my staff at 10 o'clock in the morning on Friday. I got it yesterday. Why? Because it got tangled up with all these things going on the Internet commercially... They want to deliver vast amounts of information over the Internet. And again, the Internet is not something that you just dump something on. It's not a big truck. It's a series of tubes.[1]

Clearly, Senator Stevens didn't understand the internet. But do we?

What happens when you type "google.com" and hit enter?

You probably pull up a web browser and punch "google.com" into the address bar every day. But what really happens between when you hit enter and when the familiar homepage shows up on your screen?

Website addresses

Before we talk about websites, let's talk about building addresses. Every building has an address so that people can find it easily and consistently. If we told fifty people to go to "1600 Pennsylvania Avenue Northwest, Washington, DC 20500," they'd all end up in the exact same place. Even if someone had never been in the US before, they'd be able to figure out how to get to this building: go to the District of Columbia, get onto Pennsylvania Avenue Northwest, and walk to the 1600 block.

Every webpage has its own address, just like a building. In this case, it might be *https://www.nytimes.com/section/sports*.

And just like with buildings, webpage addresses make it easy for different people to get to the same page. For instance, if you sent *https://www.nytimes.com/section/sports* to fifty friends, they'd all end up at the exact same webpage. This webpage address is called the Uniform Resource Locator, or URL.

In our example, you typed in *google.com*. But in the address bar, it says the URL is *https://www.google.com*! What's all the extra stuff?

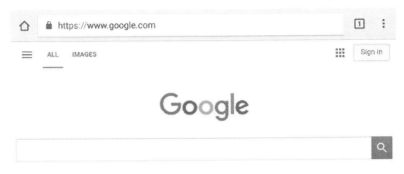

When you type in google.com, *the address bar says*
https://www.google.com. *Source: Google Chrome on Android*

To go back to our building analogy, notice that you can shorten addresses and people will still know what you mean. For instance, instead of "1600 Pennsylvania Avenue Northwest, Washington, DC 20500," you could just say "1600 Pennsylvania Avenue NW, Washington, DC," leaving out the zip code and abbreviating "northwest" to "NW." You could even just say "1600 Penn Ave NW DC" and people would still get what you mean. (Try entering all of these addresses into Google Maps — they'll all send you to the White House.)

Similarly, *google.com* is just an abbreviation of the real URL, which is *https://www.google.com*, but your browser knows what you mean and just fills in the rest of the URL.[2] But what does the rest of the URL mean, anyway?

Address decoding

When your browser sees the full URL, it breaks the URL into parts to figure out where to go. It's like how you'd break a building's address into its number, street, city, state, and zip code. Let's break down the URL like your browser would.

First is the *https://*. That's called the "protocol," and it defines how your browser should connect to the website. As an analogy, if you're trying to Uber to the White House, you have a few options for how to get there: UberPOOL, UberX, or UberBLACK (a way to ride in luxury cars).[3]

Similarly, when you're trying to get around the internet, you have a choice of two main ways of getting around, or "protocols." The default protocol is HTTP, the HyperText Transfer Protocol, which shows up as *http://* in URLs. The more secure, encrypted version of HTTP is HTTPS, the HyperText Transfer Protocol Secure, which shows up as *https://* in URLs.[4] They're pretty much the same, except HTTPS indicates that your browser should encrypt your information, which keeps it safe from hackers. If you're ever filling in a password or giving your credit card number, the website should be using HTTPS.[5] In this case, your browser knows to use HTTPS instead of HTTP — it's like telling your friend to call an UberBLACK instead of an UberX.

The second part of the URL is the *www*. It's optional for most websites, but your browser will often show it anyway for the sake of completeness.[6] It's like how, if you're giving an American phone number to another American, you don't need to give the +1 country code (as in +1-617-555-1234), but you can if you want to.

After that, your browser looks at *google.com*, which is called the "domain name." Each website has its own domain name. These should be pretty familiar: google.com, wikipedia.org, whitehouse.gov, and so on.

IP addresses

The catch is that computers don't understand domain names; they think in terms of numerical codes called IP addresses.[7] Every website has at least one IP address, like how most people have a cell phone number. Your computer can only go to websites if it knows their IP addresses. It's like how you can't just type "Bill Gates" into your phone and expect to get on the line with him — you have to look up his phone number.

To convert a domain name to an IP address, your browser uses a Domain Name Service (DNS),[8] which is like a giant address book. Your computer keeps a list of recent domain name-IP address pairs on your hard drive. If your computer can't figure out what IP address a domain name corresponds to, it'll usually ask your internet service provider (ISP), like Comcast or Verizon.[9] It's like how, if you don't have your third cousin's phone number on file, you can ask a family member who does.

Going back to our example, your computer looks up *google.com* using the DNS. Google has many IP addresses,[10] one of which is 216.58.219.206.[11]

Now your browser knows to access google.com's IP address, which could be 216.58.219.206, through secure HTTP, or HTTPS. The rest of the URL beyond the domain name, or the "path," stays the same, so *google.com/maps* would become *216.58.219.206/maps*.[12] (Here's a trick to impress your friends: type *216.58.219.206/maps* into your address bar and show them how Google Maps magically appears.)

Hold on! you might say. *We didn't specify a path; we just wanted* google.com*!* Good catch. Well, if you don't specify a path, your browser uses the placeholder path value "/", which represents the website's homepage. Both *https://www.google.com* and *https://www.google.com/* (notice the added slash in the second one) are the exact same, and both point at Google's famous homepage.

Asking Google

So, to summarize, your browser now knows to use HTTPS to grab the homepage of 216.58.219.206, an IP address that humans fondly call *google.com*. Your browser packages up this "request" and sends it to the huge computers, or "servers," that power Google's website.[13] We'll explain how exactly the information travels to Google's servers in the coming sections.

Eventually, the servers that run google.com get the request and notice that you want the homepage.[14] The servers do some computation to prepare the webpage you want. For instance, they check if there's a Google Doodle for today, in which case they'll replace the standard Google logo with the Doodle. Then, the servers gather the code to draw the homepage; this is written in languages called HTML, CSS, and JavaScript.[15]

Back to the browser

Google's servers send all this code back to your browser as a "response." Then your browser uses this code to draw the proper elements on your screen, make them look nice, and make them interactive.[16]

When you click on a link or search for something else, you'll go to a new URL, like *https://www.google.com/search?q=llama*. And thus, the cycle starts all over again.

How is sending information over the internet like shipping hot sauce?

So now we know how your computer connects to websites using the internet. But webpages, YouTube videos, and Facebook messages don't just magically teleport from a website's computers to yours.

Instead, they follow a step-by-step process. Let's explain it with an analogy — how hot sauce might get shipped to your door.

Shipping hot sauce

Say you live in Los Angeles and really like hot sauce, so you buy fifty huge bottles of hot sauce from Cholula, a company whose American branch is based right outside New York.[17]

One employee at Cholula in New York notices your order. She can't fit all fifty bottles in one box, so she separates them into ten boxes of five bottles each. To ensure you'll know if you've gotten all ten boxes, she writes "Box 1 of 10", "Box 2 of 10", etc. on the boxes. She doesn't know your address, so she just writes your name on the box.

A second employee gets your boxes from her. He notices that you have an account on Cholula's website, so he looks up your address in the database. Then he writes your address on the boxes and gives them to the post office.

The post office employee can't send your hot sauce straight from NYC to LA; that's too far a trip. Instead, the post office employee notices that there are trucks bound for Philadelphia and Chicago in the loading dock. Both of those cities are closer to LA than NYC is, so sending boxes there would be a step in the right direction. The employee can only fit 6 boxes in the Philadelphia truck, so he puts the other 4 in the Chicago truck.

When each box reaches the next city, a post office employee in that city forwards the box to any city that's a little closer to Los Angeles. From Chicago, for instance, boxes could go west to Denver or Phoenix. This continues until the boxes reach a post office that's near Los Angeles, at which point the post office just sends the boxes to LA and ultimately to your house.

The boxes take different routes to reach you, so they arrive in random order. Since the boxes are labeled, you can check to see if everything has reached. Box 3 arrives, then Box 5, then 1, 10, 8, 4, 7, 6, and 2. But wait, where's Box 9? Maybe it got lost in the mail. You ask Cholula for another box, which they send to you, and soon you have all the hot sauce you could ever want.

TCP and IP

What on earth does hot sauce have to do with the internet? As it turns out, the hot sauce shipping process we just mentioned is very similar to how information travels across the internet.

A pair of protocols, called TCP (Transmission Control Protocol) and IP (Internet Protocol), work together to send information between computers.[18] They work very similarly to the Cholula employees we just met.

Because webpages are usually too big to send all at once, TCP splits them into many little "packets" and attaches labels to each (like "1 of 10.")[19] This is like what the first Cholula employee did when she packaged all your hot sauce bottles into several smaller boxes.

Then, once it's time to send the information back to you over the internet, the servers use the Domain Name Service, or DNS, to figure out your IP address.[20] This is like how the second Cholula employee looked up your shipping address from the customer database.

Next, the information gets sent to you through the Internet Protocol. IP sends each packet across the world in several short trips, or "hops," but no matter what route the packets take, they'll reach their destination eventually.[21] That's just like how the post office sent different boxes to different intermediate points, like Philadelphia and Chicago, but the boxes eventually reached you.

Once the packets reach you, TCP reassembles them in the proper order and notices if any of them got lost, in which case it'll ask the website to send the missing packets again.[22] That's like how you used the labels on your boxes to notice that a box of hot sauce was missing.

So, in a nutshell, that's how information travels on the internet. Whether you're buying hot sauce or browsing YouTube, stuff is broken into smaller chunks (via TCP), sent to you through several intermediate shipments (via IP), and then reassembled into the original content (again via TCP).

This same process happens no matter how you're getting information over the internet. Whether you're using a web browser on your laptop to browse Facebook or using the Facebook app on your phone, information flows from Facebook's computers to yours in the exact same way. (This process even happens if you're talking to your Echo speaker or tapping your Apple Watch — again, anything that uses the internet uses this process.)

HTTP and HTTPS

You might be wondering where HTTP and HTTPS, the protocols for fetching webpages, fit into this. HTTP and HTTPS are actually built right on top of TCP and IP.[23] HTTP and HTTPS say, "get me this webpage," and TCP and IP team up to actually deliver it. In the hot sauce example, HTTP and HTTPS are like you placing the order for Cholula hot sauce. TCP is like the employee splitting up and packaging your items, and IP is like the postal service.

So while these protocols might sound obscure, they're fundamental to how you do pretty much anything online.

What path does information take from one computer to another?

Remember that, with TCP and IP, information is broken into tiny packets and sent through various intermediate computers until it reaches its destination. Each packet takes its own path from a website's servers to your computer or phone. But what do these paths look like?

To test it out, we used a Mac/Linux tool called *traceroute*, which shows the path that a sample "packet" of information took to get from your computer to a specified website.[24] We were in Washington, DC and looked up the path to ucla.edu, the website of the University of California in Los Angeles. UCLA's servers are in Los Angeles, so doing this test lets us ask: what path does information take to get from DC to LA over the internet?

You'll see the route in the below image. Each intermediate point was a computer that relayed the "packet" of information along to the next one; each trip between computers is called a "hop." It's very similar to how packages sent in the mail often stop at intermediate post offices or how you sometimes have connecting flights.

The path that a packet of information took to travel from Washington, DC to UCLA in Los Angeles. From DC, it stopped in Ashburn, VA (B); Chicago (C); Abilene, KS (D); Denver (E); Salt Lake City (F); and Las Vegas (G) before it went to UCLA. Source: traceroute and Bing Maps[25]

Notice how the packet didn't magically fly across the country. It had to travel across physical cables (which we'll talk about in the last section), so it had to obey the limitations of geography. It's interesting to note that, if you mailed a package from DC to UCLA, it might take a similar route to this packet!

It's worth noting that every packet might take a different route. Sometimes packets will bounce around the world, go backward, travel to a different country, or take all kinds of crazy detours before getting to the destination.[26]

Want to try this for yourself? Use an online *traceroute* tool[27] to look up how a packet would travel from the tool's servers to a website of your choice. You just need to provide an IP address; you can look up your own IP address[28] or try sample ones like

23.4.112.131 (mit.edu, based in Massachusetts) or 216.58.219.206 (google.com, based in northern California).

So we talked about how information travels from computer to computer over the internet. But how does information physically get from one computer to another? Read on.

Why did a Wall Street trader drill through the Allegheny Mountains to build a straight fiber-optic cable?

In 2008, a Wall Street trader named Daniel Spivey built a nearly-straight, 825-mile long fiber-optic cable between Chicago's South Loop, home to Chicago's financial exchanges, and northern New Jersey, right outside New York City and home to Nasdaq's servers. Spivey was serious about making a straight line: his work crews drilled straight through the massive Allegheny Mountains of Pennsylvania, avoiding some much easier (but slightly roundabout) routes. The price tag? $300 million.[29]

Why on earth would anyone be so obsessed with building a straight cable?

Internet cables

First, let's talk about why cables matter. Whenever information is sent across the internet through IP, it travels through long underground cables.[30] (The internet isn't a series of tubes, as Senator Ted Stevens said, but it sure is a series of cables!)

A popular type of cable is a fiber-optic cable, which you might recognize from Verizon's popular FiOS service.[31] Fiber-optic cables are made of pure glass and are no thicker than a human hair.[32] Fiber-optic cables are so clear that, if you stood on top of an ocean made of miles of solid fiber-optic glass, you'd be able to see the bottom clearly.[33]

Recall that computers store all information as 1's and 0's, just like we store text using the 26 letters of the alphabet. When your computer wants to send information to another computer (using TCP, IP, and HTTP/HTTPS), it needs to move those 1's and 0's over the cables. Your computer converts the 1's and 0's into tiny flashes of light. 1's might mean to keep the light on for a fraction of a second, while 0's might mean to keep the light off for the same amount of time. These flashes of light then travel through the fiber-optic cable. Since the fiber-optic cable is made of clear glass,[34] information can travel incredibly fast: about two-thirds the speed of light.[35]

So while information might seem to travel around the internet by magic, it actually travels through long underground cables. Since the shortest distance between two points is a straight line, the person with the straightest cables gets the fastest internet access. We all like fast internet, but who's so obsessed that they'd blast through the Alleghenies? Let's meet them.

High-frequency trading

Many "high-frequency traders," or HFTs, use software to make rapid trades between America's two major financial centers, New York and Chicago.[36] HFTs exploit tiny differences in the prices of financial assets (such as stocks and futures) between exchanges in the two cities — say, by buying a stock for $1.00 in New York and selling it for $1.01 in Chicago — to make tiny amounts of profit thousands or millions of times a day.[37] This process is called arbitrage, and arbitrage opportunities disappear quickly since they're free money. To get there first, you need a lightning-fast internet connection. It's so competitive that traders fight for edges of a few microseconds, or millionths of a second.[38]

These high-frequency traders need the fastest-possible internet connections so they can beat their competitors to the lucrative trades. Since information travels across the internet in giant cables, traders need the straightest possible cables.[39]

That brings us back to the question: why did the trader Daniel Spivey spend so much money building an incredibly straight cable? It's to maximize the internet speed between the two financial capitals, which would help HFTs get an edge. The cable was far straighter than the previous record holder: Spivey's cable sends information between New York and Chicago in just 13 milliseconds, a full 3 milliseconds faster than the previous record.[40] HFTs were willing to spend top dollar for this slight speed advantage: the first 200 HFTs to sign up to use this cable spent a combined $2.8 billion.[41]

Remember how fiber-optic cables let information travel at two-thirds the speed of light? That's still too slow for some traders. In 2014, one company started experimenting with giant laser guns that would beam information through the air between NYC and Chicago. Since light travels faster through air than glass, information would travel far faster — and it would probably be near-impossible to beat.[42]

But for now, at least, cables are the way to go. And as long as we'll have cables, we'll have mildly obsessive Wall Street traders like Daniel Spivey.

Chapter 5.
Cloud Computing

As recently as the early 2000s, you would go to Blockbuster to rent movies, buy Photoshop and Microsoft Office in boxes from Best Buy, and store your company's files in a massive computer room at your headquarters. Nowadays, you binge movies online with Netflix, pay monthly subscription fees for Photoshop and all manner of other apps, and store your company's files in far-flung mega-computers with services like Dropbox or Amazon Web Services.

It turns out that all three of these changes have something in common. It's called the cloud, and it has nothing to do with the weather. So what is it? Let's take a look.

How is Google Drive like Uber?

Owning a car gets expensive: between fuel, insurance, repairs, taxes, and other costs, you'll have to fork over $8,000 a year.[1] But if you want the freedom to get around, you have no choice but to own a car.

Or do you?

Ridesharing apps like Uber, Lyft, and Zipcar solve this problem by letting you rent cars on demand. Since you pay per ride, Uber is a great deal if you don't drive much: Uber is cheaper than owning a car if you drive less than 9,500 miles a year.[2] You can call an Uber pretty much anytime, anywhere, whereas if you owned a car you have to be with it to use it. And, with Uber, you don't have to worry about repairs, gas, or car theft, since you don't own the cars you're riding in.[3]

What does this have to do with technology? Well, technology is undergoing a shift that parallels the owning-to-Uber shift in cars.[4]

Traditional vs. cloud computing

Traditionally, you'd buy apps like Microsoft Word and store files on your own laptop. It's like owning a car: you'd get full control but full responsibility as well. If your hard drive broke or if you lost your laptop, you'd be out of luck, much like you'd be in trouble if your car goes bust or gets stolen. And you'd pay a flat fee no matter how much you use — whether you're a hardcore writer or just a note-taker, you'd pay the same amount for Word.

Meanwhile, since the mid-2000s, you've been able to run apps like Google Docs in your web browser and store your files online with Google Drive. Files you keep in Google Drive can be run anywhere, on any internet-connected device, and you can run Google Docs on any browser or phone as long as you log into your account. So even if your laptop gets run over by a truck, you can borrow anyone's computer, log in, and access your files like nothing even happened. And you only pay for as much as you need: Google Drive gives you 15 GB of storage for free, and you can pay a few extra bucks for more space.[5] In short, it's like Uber: access your stuff anywhere, own nothing, and pay for only what you need.

This new model of computing, where you store your apps and files online instead of on your own laptop, is called "cloud computing" or "the cloud."[6] Microsoft Word and hard drives are traditional computing, while Google Docs and Google Drive are cloud computing.

To go back to the analogy, cloud computing is like Uber for computers.[7] Instead of owning your own car or computer, you can get your files or transportation on-demand from anywhere with an internet connection.

Cloud computing is everywhere. Gmail is a classic example: you access your emails from a web interface instead of, say, the Microsoft Outlook app.[8] Spotify lets you listen to music over the internet instead of downloading and owning songs. Your iPhone stores your texts and other files on Apple's iCloud so that they all come back even when you switch to a new phone. And so on.

Where do things in "the cloud" live?

When you visit Google Drive in your browser, your files show up as if by magic. You can tap a button on Spotify and music will start playing. But all computer files — from spreadsheets to songs — must exist as 0's and 1's on a computer somewhere. But if these files aren't on your computer, where are they?

Technologists will tell you that this information lives "in the cloud," but that's not that helpful.[9] Obviously, there are no giant floating computers in the sky that store your data. What does this weird buzzword mean?

Data centers

Simply put: "the cloud" is just someone else's computer. When you make a Google Doc on Google Drive, all your text and photos are stored on Google's computers instead of your own. Whenever you run Gmail, the email processing is also done on Google's computers instead of your own.

Now, when we say "Google's computers," we don't mean some Google employee's laptop. Instead, Google Docs lives on Google's "servers," which are powerful computers that specialize in storing data and running apps and websites. Servers are used only for their computational might, so they usually lack keyboards, mice, screens, and apps like iTunes or Chrome. Servers also don't shut down (not intentionally, at least), since services like Google Drive and Gmail need to run 24/7.[10]

Servers are often stored in huge buildings called "data centers," which feature racks and racks of stacked servers (the collection of servers is colorfully called a "server farm"). Data centers can't be any old building, though. Data centers need to have powerful cooling systems, since servers get extremely hot. Data centers also need backup electrical generators in case the power goes out.[11]

A view inside a data center, with many servers — computers that run websites and apps — in the foreground. Source: Torkild Retvedt[12]

Frontends and backends

These servers do a lot of the computation that apps and websites demand. Whenever you log into Google Docs to view your document, Google retrieves your data from its servers and shows it to you. Similarly, Spotify's music files live on servers that Spotify has rented out.[13] Whenever you want to play a song on Spotify, your web browser sends a message to the Spotify servers asking for the song. Spotify's servers send back the song file, and your web browser plays it.[14] Your Spotify app or browser tab is called the "frontend," and Spotify's servers are called the "backend."[15]

Backends are generally more secure than frontends because the app makers get tighter control over what happens in the backend, whereas users get more control over the frontend. So anything that involves passwords or databases tends to happen on servers,[16] whereas interactive user interfaces are usually drawn by the frontend.[17] For instance, all of the Gmail code to send, receive, and search through emails runs on Google's servers; the buttons you click in your web browser just tell the servers what to do.[18]

The best and worst of the cloud

So cloud computing is just storing files and running apps on distant companies' servers. It's tremendously convenient: with Dropbox, for instance, you don't need to email files to yourself, and your files will be safe even if your laptop gets mauled by a gorilla.[19] But what are the risks?

One is security: the moment you put your files on someone else's computer, you're trusting them to keep your stuff safe. Sometimes your stuff isn't kept safe: in 2014, hackers broke into user accounts on iCloud, Apple's online backup service (similar to Dropbox), and leaked nude photos of several Hollywood actors.[20]

But Apple worked hard to improve its security,[21] and most cloud providers today have incredibly tough security. For instance, when a hard drive at a Google data center gets decommissioned, employees ruthlessly crush and shred it so no one can get the information stored on it. Google's data centers also have "custom-designed electronic access cards, alarms, vehicle access barriers, perimeter fencing, metal detectors, and biometrics" to prevent intruders from breaking in. Their data center floors even have "laser beam intrusion detection,"[22] the kind of thing you'd expect to see in a James Bond movie. Simply put, cloud companies do a lot to keep your information secure, and your information is probably safer in the cloud than on your computer.[23]

A second troubling concern is around privacy: if you store your stuff on someone else's computer, you can only hope that they don't let anyone read it.[24] These are legitimate fears. American courts have tried several times to force Google and Microsoft to hand over emails stored on their servers.[25] To their credit, Microsoft[26] and Google[27] have repeatedly pushed back against these demands.

And the third issue is around internet access. If all your favorite apps — like Twitter and Google Maps — are web apps, then you can't be very productive if you aren't connected to the internet (say, when you're on a plane with exorbitantly expensive Wi-Fi).[28] However, many apps have been making progress on working offline. Google Docs and Gmail now offer limited functionality offline,[29] and several games and productivity apps have made offline-capable versions through Google Chrome.[30]

So, while there are some risks, the convenience and security of cloud storage make it an overall strong choice.

Why can't you own Photoshop anymore?

In 1990, Adobe launched the first version of its famous photo-editing tool Photoshop. You could buy a floppy disk containing the software from a computer or hobbyist store.[31] Eventually, Adobe upgraded to CDs, and later you could download the software directly.[32] But no matter how you installed the app, you would pay for this "perpetual license" to use the software — meaning that the app was all yours, to keep and use forever.[33] Photoshop CS6, released in 2012, was $700.[34]

The box that the first version of Adobe Photoshop, released in 1990, came in, as well as the floppy disk the software lived on. Source: ComputerHistory[35]

But in 2013, Adobe announced a massive shift: you would no longer be able to own any of its "Creative Suite" apps, including Photoshop. Instead, you could download Photoshop for free, but you'd have to subscribe to their new Creative Cloud service, which cost about $20 a month, to keep using it.[36] This new model of "renting" Photoshop is called software-as-a-service, or SaaS (pronounced like *sass*).[37] It's like leasing a car instead of buying it.

Here's how it works. Once you've downloaded Photoshop, you need to enter a license key. Then the app connects to Adobe's servers to check that your license key is valid, and it'll do this every month to ensure that you've been paying.[38] Note that Photoshop still runs entirely on your computer; only checking your subscription uses the cloud.[39] But if your subscription expires, sorry — Photoshop will refuse to work!

What was in it for Adobe

Moving to a subscription model for Photoshop (also known as a software-as-a-service model) proved to be a smart business move for Adobe. For one, they could earn more consistent revenue, since they started getting subscription fees every month instead of having to wait for a huge new release, which only happens once every few years.[40] It also helped Adobe fight piracy, since the monthly license check means that Adobe gets to decide who can and can't use the software.[41] And third, since Photoshop now regularly connects to the internet, Adobe can constantly push updates and bug fixes instead of having to wait until the next big version is ready. This keeps customers happy and helps squash security issues faster.[42] (This development model is called "agile development.")

This move wasn't without controversy, though.

Customer complaints

Customers weren't happy at the time. Many were angry that Adobe was forcing users to upgrade, and they felt Adobe was trying to milk them for money by making them keep paying for Photoshop forever.[43] A prominent blogger called the move "the biggest money grab in the history of software,"[44] and consumer advocates called it "predatory."[45]

But it turns out that consumers quickly got over their anger, adopting cloud Photoshop in droves[46]: Adobe's revenue jumped 70% within a year.[47] Why? For one, a subscription lets you get continuous updates for no extra cost.[48] Second, it makes Photoshop more accessible for new users. You now get a month-long free trial, and the first year costs $240, compared to $700 to buy the last boxed version.[49] Third, Creative Cloud lets you store your Photoshop files in the cloud for no extra cost, making it easy to edit on any of your devices.[50]

So despite the original controversy, moving to a subscription service was huge for Adobe: it helped double Adobe's stock price and boost revenue 70% in just one year.[51]

Slow adoption

You might be wondering why, if offering Photoshop as a subscription service (or software-as-a-service) is so great, it took Adobe 22 years (from 1990 to 2012) to discover it.

First, it's important to note that the software-as-a-service model relies entirely on the internet, so people will only buy subscriptions if they have internet access. These days, we often take it for granted that everyone has internet access, but that hasn't always been true. In 1997, only 18% of Americans had internet access at home, but that number had quadrupled to 72% by 2011,[52] which made it much more feasible to start selling software solely over the internet.

The second reason it took so long is that Adobe's cloud platform, Creative Cloud, took several years for engineers to build. Creative Cloud wasn't announced until 2011,[53] and only after this could Photoshop move to the subscription model.

Other examples of SaaS

We've talked a lot about the Photoshop example, but it's important to note that this business model is widespread. Remember that SaaS stands for software-as-a-service, which is a business model where customers buy subscriptions for software to be delivered over the internet.[54] Many times SaaS apps run online, but not always — recall that, even with the subscription model, the Photoshop app still runs on your own machine.[55]

There are plenty of other examples of SaaS. Dropbox lets you rent out one terabyte of storage on their servers for a few dollars a month.[56] Spotify lets you play unlimited music for a monthly price.[57] Gmail is free for individuals, but companies can pay to get unlimited web-based email through G Suite.[58] Google Sheets, the SaaS version of Microsoft Excel, is also free, but you can pay a few bucks a month to get extra file storage on Google Drive.[59]

What do all these examples of SaaS apps have in common? You can access all these apps through a web browser, and all your data is stored on other companies' servers. In other words, SaaS is just another name for apps that run in the cloud.[60]

That brings us back to the question we asked at the start: why can't you own Photoshop anymore? Photoshop has evolved into a SaaS app, and as such you can only rent it. Start thinking about the apps you use every day, and you'll start seeing more and more examples of SaaS.

Why did Microsoft run ads making fun of Office?

In 2019, Microsoft ran a strange series of ads comparing its newly-released Office 2019, which you buy once and use forever without future updates, to Office 365, which you subscribe to for a steady stream of updates and bonus features.[61]

These ads showed a set of twins, one given a 2019 version of an Office app (like Excel) and the other given a 365 version. The twins had to complete identical tasks — in every case, the 365 twin finished faster thanks to Office 365's special features and had time to jump rope, dice peppers, or blend smoothies.[62]

So why would Microsoft make fun of its own products this way?

"Frozen in time"

Office 2019 offers "frozen-in-time" versions of Microsoft's classic productivity apps, including Word and PowerPoint. It follows the traditional model of computing: buy it once and own it, in exchange for never getting updates.[63] Office 2019 was, at the time, the latest in a long line of traditionally-licensed Office versions, which were usually released every three years. (Before 2010, these "frozen-in-time" versions were the only ways to get Office.[64])

Meanwhile, Office 365 is software-as-a-service. You pay yearly and get constant upgrades plus artificial intelligence (AI) assistance, special features on mobile apps, and free storage on Microsoft's cloud storage system, OneDrive.[65]

As you can imagine, Microsoft was trying to tell users that Office 365 was better than Office 2019. Indeed, the bonus features and constant upgrades are great for consumers. But the main reason Microsoft was pushing Office 365 was that Microsoft makes tons of money from 365[66] — more than from "frozen-in-time" versions.[67] That's probably because, on 365, a customer keeps paying by default and has to make an active choice to cancel — versus with "frozen-in-time" versions, the customer stays with the old version by default and has to make the active choice to upgrade (and pay). In other words, the path of least resistance for 365 users (but not for "frozen-in-time" users) is to keep paying, so of course most keep paying.

The benefits for Office 365 go further. Once Microsoft has signed a company up for this subscription service, it can easily upsell other subscription services like Azure.[68] Microsoft can also push other cloud-based productivity tools like Teams, a corporate messaging app, to Office 365 subscribers, which keeps customers locked into the Microsoft ecosystem.[69]

Why both?

The obvious question, then, is why Microsoft keeps the "frozen-in-time" versions of Office around if it so obviously prefers 365. We think it's because Microsoft notices that some users are still resistant to the idea of subscription software[70] and wants to avoid the fallout of forcing users to switch. By slowly phasing out the "legacy" frozen-in-time Office versions, Microsoft can keep customers happy in the short term as it slowly moves people to the more lucrative Office 365.

How does Amazon Web Services work?

We've talked a lot about software-as-a-service, or SaaS, which is an increasingly popular model for consumer software like Google Docs or Spotify. But that's just part of the story. Big businesses and tech companies have tons of data and users, and they're also turning to the cloud.

If you're running a big website or app, you'll need a huge server to handle all the data and computation. But unlike consumer-focused laptops and phones, servers aren't always the cheapest or easiest to set up and maintain. To set up your own server, you have to buy machines, mess around with IP addresses, install complex server software like Apache, keep the computers cool (this is a harder problem than you think[71]), and keep software updated and running.[72] Sometimes you even need to hire dedicated specialists to keep your servers working.[73] Simply put, it's a pain.

Instead, what if you just rented out a server and avoided all those hassles? (It's like getting around with Uber instead of trying to buy and maintain a car yourself.) Thanks to tools called cloud computing services, you can.

The most famous of these cloud computing services is Amazon Web Services, or AWS, which lets you rent out Amazon's servers instead of buying your own.[74] Amazon Web Services is actually a family of applications, the biggest of which are the Elastic Compute Cloud (EC2) and Simple Storage Service (S3).[75] In a nutshell, EC2 lets you run your app's code on Amazon servers,[76] while S3 lets you store all your app's data on those servers.[77]

All of Amazon's own products run on AWS — whenever you buy something on Amazon.com, you're using a website that's built on S3 and EC2. In fact, AWS was originally created when, in 2000, Amazon needed to build a common box of tools for all its internal software development teams to use. Amazon later realized that other companies might want to use these tools too, so in 2006 they spun them off into AWS.[78] In short, when you use AWS to build an app, you're borrowing the same tools that Amazon has used to build its own gigantic operations.

Benefits of the cloud

As we hinted at earlier, renting servers with Amazon Web Services is far easier than running your own servers, since Amazon will take care of upgrades, security, and other maintenance issues. Amazon owns millions of servers, which their customers share; each customer gets (and pays for) only as many servers as they need. Plus, since Amazon has so many servers, they have achieved great economics of scale, which drives the cost of a server down.[79] The cost savings really can be massive: one health research startup would have paid $1 million for their own servers, but instead chose AWS and only has to pay $25,000 a month.[80]

A second big reason is security. Sony, Target, and Home Depot all avoided the security features of Amazon Web Services, instead choosing to run their own servers — but all three companies were victims of data breaches, where hackers broke into their servers and stole customer data.[81] (Think about it: would Amazon or the Home Depot have more online security experts on staff?)

A third reason is reliability. Businesses can't make money if their websites or apps are down, and fortunately cloud computing providers like AWS are excellent at keeping their servers running. AWS keeps multiple copies of apps and data on several independent data centers around the world, so your app will be fine even if a natural disaster strikes one data center or a few servers break down.[82] Meanwhile, if you ran your own servers, you'd just have to hope that your one data center is safe. As Investopedia puts it, "Imagine if Netflix were to have all of their personnel files, their content and their backed-up data centralized on-site on the eve of a hurricane. It would be madness."[83] Using cloud platforms like AWS helps Netflix keep its chill.

SaaS, IaaS, and PaaS

AWS isn't the only game in town, though it does control more of the market than anyone else, with 34% market share in the cloud computing services space — three times more than its nearest competitor.[84] That competitor is a Microsoft product called Azure. Google also competes in this space with its Google Cloud Platform.[85] All these platforms let app developers use the same technology that the companies' own apps use; for instance, YouTube runs on the Google Cloud Platform, and so can anyone else's app.[86]

Remember how SaaS refers to rentable web apps? Technologists have acronyms for these cloud computing providers as well. AWS, Azure, and Google Cloud Platform are all infrastructure-as-a-service (IaaS; we have no idea how to pronounce it), which lets app makers borrow servers to run their apps on.[87]

There's a third kind of cloud service that falls somewhere between IaaS and SaaS: platform-as-a-service (PaaS, pronounced like *pass*).[88] These platforms often include extra useful features like databases, advanced analytics, and entire operating systems.[89] Basically, PaaS makes it even easier for developers to build websites in the cloud. PaaS examples aren't as famous, but one is Heroku, a service that lets you just send in your app's code and then automatically sets up the website, with minimal setup required.[90] (AWS, which is IaaS, also makes it easy to set up a website, but PaaS makes it even easier.)

What's the difference between SaaS, IaaS, and PaaS? Let's use an analogy: food. SaaS is like a restaurant: you just tell the waiter what food you want, and they'll bring it to you. IaaS is like renting a kitchen: you have the space, but you have to bring your own ingredients and utensils and cook the food yourself. PaaS sits in between SaaS and IaaS: you give someone your ingredients and recipe, and they'll prepare the food for you.

To summarize, what's Amazon Web Services? In a word, it's IaaS. But, in plain English, it's a tool that lets you rent space on Amazon's servers, making it much faster, cheaper, and easier to launch an app than if you had to set up your own servers.

How does Netflix handle sudden spikes in viewership when a new show launches?

One Sunday in March 2015, Netflix aired the premiere of the third season of the wildly-popular show *House of Cards*, and people flocked to see it: Netflix's traffic that day was 30% higher than on a normal Sunday.[91] This 30% jump is huge, especially when you consider that, in 2015, Netflix accounted for 37% of all internet traffic.[92] (This wasn't a one-off incident, either: HBO saw a 300% spike in traffic when the fifth season of *Game of Thrones* premiered in April 2015.[93]) How did Netflix's website handle such a huge influx of visitors?

First, let's look at how Netflix runs its website. In 2008, Netflix owned its own servers, but over the next several years, it started moving more and more of its website to Amazon Web Services, finishing the job in 2016.[94] The cloud offers Netflix three main benefits over owning their own servers. Let's start with one feature called "elasticity."

Elasticity

When Netflix owned its own servers, it had to have enough servers to handle peak usage. The problem was that, most of the time, usage wasn't at its peak, so most of the servers would be sitting around unused — which meant wasted money.[95] But cloud hosting services like Amazon Web Services will instantly grow or shrink the computing power given to your app as your app's usage goes up or down during the day, so you only pay for as much usage as you need.[96] This is elasticity.

As an analogy, imagine you owned a restaurant that had a huge lunch rush but only had a trickle of customers at every other time. If all your employees had to work the same hours, you'd need to hire enough to handle the lunch rush — but then, for the rest of the day, you'd have way too many people doing nothing but eating up your payroll. But if you could flexibly adjust your employees' shifts, you could bring in more employees during the busy times and send home the extra employees during quiet times. That way you'd only pay for as much as you need.

All apps can save money with elasticity, but Netflix in particular benefits a lot because its usage varies a great amount throughout the day. Not many people watch Netflix from 9-5, but viewership peaks at around 10pm every night.[97] Thanks to its elasticity, Amazon Web Services can automatically give Netflix more or less computing power throughout the day, instead of having the same amount all day.[98]

Scalability

Besides elasticity, why else would Netflix move to the cloud? One big reason is "scalability": Amazon Web Services helps you grow, or scale, your application quickly as you get more users (this is growth on the scale of months and years, not sudden spikes).[99] This is quite important for Netflix because the amount of video viewed on Netflix grew over 1,000-fold from 2007 to 2015.[100] Without the cloud, Netflix would have had to physically install new servers all the time, but Amazon Web Services automatically gave them more computing power as they grew, with no work needed on Netflix's end.[101]

Redundancy

The last big reason why Netflix chose the cloud was because Amazon Web Services was more reliable than owning their own data centers, or buildings full of servers.[102] This is primarily because the cloud builds in lots of "redundancy," or multiple copies of the same information or code. Even if a few computers fail, there will be plenty of others to pick up the slack.[103] (It's like how we humans only need one kidney but have two, so that even if one fails — or we donate one! — we're fine.[104])

The cloud gives Netflix some huge advantages, but it wasn't a simple change. It took Netflix seven years to completely migrate from their own servers to Amazon Web Services — and, along the way, they basically had to rebuild all their infrastructure and databases from scratch.[105] It was a lot of work, but it will probably be worth it in the end.

So the next time you're binge watching Netflix, thank the engineers who decided to move to the cloud. (Your friends who haven't read this book might be confused by your sudden fascination with the sky, but tell them not to worry and just enjoy the show.)

How did a single typo take down 20% of the internet?

The date was February 28, 2017.[106] An Amazon engineer typed in a standard command to disable a few Amazon Web Services servers to fix a billing issue. But the engineer made a typo that accidentally took down a huge amount of servers, which forced AWS to restart S3.[107] You'll recall that S3 lets developers store photos, videos, and other files in the cloud — think of it like a massive Dropbox for apps.[108] For the next four hours,[109] nearly 20% of the internet was down, including popular sites like Medium, Quora,[110] Netflix, Spotify, and Pinterest.[111] The damage was extensive: S&P 500 companies lost over $150 million.[112]

How did this happen?

The answer: the affected sites all relied on Amazon Web Services.[113] Their code ran on Amazon servers and their files lived on Amazon servers (specifically, S3). So when Amazon Web Services' servers went down, all the sites went down as well.

This highlights one of the biggest pitfalls of cloud computing: if you run your app in the cloud, you're in trouble whenever your provider has an "outage."[114] Even the best cloud providers won't have 100% "uptime."[115] For instance, Amazon Web Services was down for a total of two and a half hours in 2015, which means it was up about 99.97% of the time.[116] (The world is so unpredictable that it's impossible to anticipate every potential point of server failure — and even if you did, it'd get too expensive.[117] It's like how Disney World in Florida could prepare for a snowstorm — it has snowed there before[118] — but it's so unlikely that it's not worth the expense.)

So what can app makers do about the inevitable downtime of cloud hosting providers? Well, they could buy their own servers and run their apps on those servers, a model known as "on-premises" or "on-prem."[119] While this would let companies put matters into their own hands, the numbers suggest that it might backfire. For instance, Microsoft offers two ways for companies to get enterprise email: in the cloud with Office 365 or on-premises with Exchange. One study found that Exchange was down almost 3.5 times as much as Office 365, which equals an extra nine hours of downtime every year.[120]

If on-premises computing is worse than the cloud, app makers' best choice might just be to use the cloud and accept that occasional failure is inevitable. Cloud service providers like Amazon Web Services and Microsoft Azure, for their part, should tell customers immediately when their servers go down, work fast to fix the problem, and do their best to ensure it doesn't happen again.[121]

As an example of how (and how not) to deal with outages, let's quickly go back to the story of the Amazon Web Services typo. AWS was criticized because, during the outage, its dashboard showed that everything was fine — ironically because the dashboard ran on AWS itself and went down as well.[122] But to their credit, Amazon has put in security checks to limit the damage that these kind of typos can do, and it did extensive safety checks throughout the system.[123]

That brings us back to our original question: how did a single typo take down 20% of the internet? Well, that 20% of the internet ran on Amazon Web Services, and when AWS had to restart because of that fateful typo, the websites that ran on AWS went down as well.

But, for all its flaws, the cloud is a great tool to save money, improve website reliability, and scale sites up more quickly. And it makes consumers' lives much more convenient, as well. So yes, this time it's OK to have your head in the clouds.

Chapter 6.
Big Data

We humans generate a mind-boggling amount of data. As Google cofounder Eric Schmidt put it in 2010, "every two days now we create as much information as we did from the dawn of civilization up until 2003."[1] That is, we create five exabytes, or five trillion GB, of data every two days.[2] That's like if every person on Earth filled up a 512GB iPhone every single day.[3] (And mind you, this quote was way back in 2010!)

This is an enormous amount of data. It's huge, colossal, titanic. Or, as technologists call it, "big." Companies are using big data to reinvent technology and themselves, to the point where one analyst said that "information is the oil of the 21st century."[4] But how?

How did Target know that a teenager was pregnant before her own father did?

In 2012, a father in Minnesota was surprised to find coupons for maternity goods from Target in the mail — and he was furious to see that they were addressed to his teenage daughter. He stormed into the nearest Target and confronted a confused Target manager, demanding to know if the manager was trying to encourage his impressionable young daughter to get pregnant. Naturally, the manager apologized. He even followed up on the phone a few days later to apologize again.[5]

On the phone, though, the father sounded embarrassed. "I had a talk with my daughter," he said. "It turns out there's been some activities in my house I haven't been completely aware of. She's due in August. I owe you an apology."[6]

Target had figured out that this teenager was pregnant before her own father did![7] But how? The answer: big data.

Retailers know that major life events like going to college or starting a new job tend to lead to new buying habits, which they are eager to take advantage of.[8] For instance, Gillette sends teenage boys free razors on their 18th birthdays.[9] Similarly, pregnancy is a pivotal moment for retailers because new mothers start needing things like baby clothes and formula, spending hundreds of dollars along the way.[10] But because birth records are usually public, new parents get overwhelmed with offers from retailers trying to get their business. To stand out, retailers like Target need to preempt birth and start reaching expecting mothers as early as the second trimester, when they start needing things like maternity clothes and prenatal vitamins.[11]

Thus, retailers need to predict and pre-empt pregnancy or other situations that cause new buying habits. To do this, they try to find patterns in the data they gather about customers.[12] For instance, suppose you notice that customers with 18-year-old children tend to buy a lot of dorm room furniture in the fall, probably because their kids are moving into college. Then you could start sending coupons for furniture and school supplies to people with 18-year-old kids every summer to pre-empt the fall move-in. That's more likely to lead to a sale than sending random people these coupons.

Getting to know you

But how do stores collect all this data? Many use free "loyalty cards" or "savings cards," which they scan when you check out. By tracking your buying habits this way, they can create targeted offers for you.[13] However, two of the biggest retailers, Walmart and Target, have no such card. Instead, Target[14] and Walmart[15] assign each credit card a unique code, which they can track to understand a customer's purchase history and start targeting coupons. Internally, Target calls their code the "Guest ID number."[16]

It's not just purchases, though. Target can link a lot more information to your Guest ID:

> "If you use a credit card or a coupon, or fill out a survey, or mail in a refund, or call the customer help line, or open an e-mail we've sent you or visit our Web

site, we'll record it and link it to your Guest ID," said Andrew Pole, Target's Director of Guest Data.[17]

Demographic information like your age, ethnicity, and address are also tied to your Guest ID. Target could also try to guess your salary, perhaps by finding the estimated price of your home, and they could use public records to learn when your kids were born, when you got married, and even if you got divorced.[18]

Predicting pregnancy

As you can imagine, Target compiles huge amounts of information on each Guest ID. Using this data, Target can start finding patterns and making predictions about customer behavior. For instance, Target found that women who suddenly bought large amounts of unscented lotion were likely around the beginning of their second trimester, because these purchases tended to correlate with births a few months later. Pregnant women were also likely to buy supplements like zinc, calcium, and magnesium.[19]

Eventually, Target identified a group of roughly 25 buying habits that, when analyzed together, would let the company assign each shopper a "pregnancy prediction" score. With this "predictive analytics" solution, Target can predict pregnancy with 87% confidence — and sometimes, they can even predict the approximate date of delivery.[20] As the example from Minnesota shows, Target might even know soon-to-be moms better than their own parents!

Techniques like this helped Target's "Mom & Baby" section grow quickly and boosted Target's overall revenue.[21] But the challenge for retailers like Target is capitalizing on these customer insights without coming across as "creepy." As you might expect, many couples were startled when Target sent them targeted pregnancy coupons shortly after they realized they were expecting. Some were so startled, in fact, that they stopped visiting Target altogether. Thus, Target started getting subtler with its promotions. The company would still send prenatal vitamin coupons, but they would be nestled between, say, a charcoal coupon and a lawnmower ad to make these targeted ads appear "random."[22]

Retailers don't just use gut instinct to guess what their customers would want. In the era of big data, they're using cold, hard numbers to figure that out.

How do Google and other major companies analyze big data?

As we mentioned, Target has data on hundreds of millions of customers.[23] But how can they analyze this data to create metrics like the pregnancy prediction score? It's not like some analyst can just pop open an Excel file on her laptop. The data is too massive to store or analyze on a single computer, even the most powerful ones.[24] Imagine trying to multiply two 500-digit numbers on a four-function pocket calculator — no matter how good your calculator might be, a single calculator can't do it.

It'd be far too expensive to make a supercomputer powerful or big enough to handle all this data itself. Instead, the key is to break your data and computation into more manageable chunks, which you assign to an army of cheap, normal-sized computers. All these computers can work simultaneously, and once the last computer is done, you just combine their results into a final answer.[25]

As an analogy, imagine you want to count every person in your city. You could run around counting everyone yourself, but that would take far too long. Instead, you send one friend to each neighborhood and tell them to count all the people they see in that small area. Each friend reports their count to you, and when the last friend gives you their count, you just have to add the totals together to get your answer.[26] This is far faster than counting by yourself, since your friends work on much smaller, and shorter, tasks "in parallel." (Fun fact: this is how the Roman Empire ran its censuses![27])

MapReduce

Google uses this strategy for its famous "MapReduce" algorithms:[28] the "Map" step is when your friends counted each neighborhood, and the "Reduce" step is when you added up your friends' results.

The popular big data tool Hadoop uses MapReduce.[29] The idea is that you store all your data on a bunch of normal-sized servers — no supercomputers needed! — and then run the Hadoop software to crunch the numbers. The beauty of this approach is that the computers don't need to be physically connected, and to add more data you just need to add more computers.[30] Hadoop is quickly becoming an industry standard. Besides Target,[31] companies like Netflix,[32] eBay,[33] Facebook,[34] and many more use Hadoop. In fact, one analysis predicted that 80% of the Fortune 500 would be using Hadoop by 2020.[35]

In short, analyzing big data is far more complex than just using Excel: there are specialized tools and techniques that you need to use. Big data analysis is so rigorous and important that it spawned a whole new field of study: data science.[36]

Why do prices on Amazon change every 10 minutes?

Not a fan of the price of an item on Amazon? Just wait 10 minutes. It might just change.

Amazon changes product prices 2.5 million times a day,[37] meaning that an average product listed on Amazon changes prices every 10 minutes.[38] That's fifty times more often than Walmart and Best Buy![39] The constant price changes have annoyed some consumers when they see the price of an item drop right after they buy it,[40] but they've also helped Amazon boost profits by 25%.[41]

How do they do it? Amazon has, simply put, tons of data. They have 1.5 billion items listed for sale and 200 million users. Amazon has one billion gigabytes of data on their items and users.[42] If you put all that data on 500-gigabyte hard drives and stacked them up, the pile of hard drives would be over eight times as tall as Mount Everest.[43] Now that's some big data.

With all this data, Amazon analyzes customer's shopping patterns, competitors' prices, profit margins, inventory, and a dizzying array of other factors every 10 minutes to choose new prices for its products.[44] This way they can ensure their prices are always competitive and squeeze out ever more profit.[45]

Through this process, one useful strategy Amazon has found is to undercut their competitors on popular products but actually raise the prices on uncommon products, such as by discounting bestsellers while jacking up prices on obscure books. The idea is that most people will just search for the most common products (which will end up being cheaper on Amazon), so they'll start to assume that Amazon has the best prices overall. That'll hook customers on Amazon and get them to pay more for the less-common things they'll buy down the road.[46]

Data-driven suggestions

Frequently bought together

Amazon's "Frequently bought together" section uses past shoppers' purchase history to recommend items to you. Source: Amazon

There are plenty of other ways Amazon uses its data about you to make a buck. Based on your and other customers' purchase history, Amazon can bombard you with recommendations

— look no further than the "Inspired by Your Browsing History" or "Customers Who Bought This Item Also Bought" sections you see around Amazon.[47] Amazon can even use the words you highlight on the Kindle to predict what you're going to buy.[48]

Amazon makes these recommendations by finding patterns in past customers' purchases. For instance, suppose Amazon noticed that millions of customers buy peanut butter, jelly, and bread together. Then, say you buy peanut butter and bread off Amazon. Using the pattern that it's found, Amazon could suggest you buy jelly.[49]

Predicting what you want to buy goes far beyond just recommended purchases, though. Consider Amazon's patented technique called the "Anticipatory Shipping Model."[50] When Amazon predicts that you're going to buy something (like how Target predicts when women are going to deliver their babies), they can ship that item to a warehouse near you, so that when you ultimately buy it, they'll get to you quickly and cheaply.[51]

As you can see, big data has tremendous economic value — so much, in fact, that the New York Times once compared it favorably to gold.[52]

Is it good or bad that companies have so much data?

Usually, when companies use big data to become more efficient, nobody complains. For instance, no one minded when UPS used the data they collected from sensors on their trucks to optimize their delivery routes, saving $50 million. (Some people actually praised UPS for saving gas![53])

But controversy arises when companies collect personal data, like when retailers such as Target start gathering enormous volumes of data on customers.[54] Big data lets companies create targeted ads and recommendations, which can be very profitable. Google and Facebook rely on targeted ads for most of their revenue,[55] and Netflix says its recommendation system saves them $1 billion a year by keeping users on the platform (recruiting new users is very expensive).[56] But does this help the consumer?

On one hand, targeted ads and recommendations can be useful for consumers. While Target might make money by sending you targeted coupons, the coupons might save you time and money. Even though Netflix has a shocking amount of information on everything you've watched, Netflix's movie and TV show recommendations are very popular.[57]

On the other hand, privacy advocates are outraged by how much personal information big companies are collecting about you.[58] Remember how Target can figure out your marital status, address, and estimated salary — things you probably wouldn't tell a stranger off the street.[59] And if a company that has so much personal data gets hacked, the consequences can be dangerous. In 2013, thieves stole 40 million Target customers' credit card numbers and 70 million customers' personal information, including names, emails, and mailing addresses. Those 70 million customers were at high risk of identity theft.[60] And it's not just Target: all of Yahoo's 3 billion accounts were hacked in 2013, letting thieves steal birthdates and phone numbers,[61] and in 2017 hackers got access to 143 million Americans' social security numbers when they hacked the credit reporting agency Equifax.[62]

But many companies argue that they're protecting people's identities by anonymizing data, but even anonymous data could be used to reverse engineer your identity, also known as "reidentifying" you.[63] For instance, an MIT study found that just knowing the dates and locations of four credit card purchases was enough to determine the identities of 90% of people tested.[64] Another study found that you could reidentify people by mashing up anonymous user data from Netflix and IMDb.[65]

So is big data good or bad for society? Like many things about technology, there's no black-or-white answer. While big data makes companies and products more effective, it can create problems for privacy. But whether or not you like it, big data will only keep getting bigger.

Chapter 7.
Hacking & Security

Gone are the days where wannabe Nigerian princes would email you about "large amounts of money" they needed your help transferring — a ploy they said would earn you a commission but would actually let them drain your bank account.[1] Hackers have become far more competent and subtle.

So what are the newest additions to online criminals' bag of tricks? And what can we do about them?

How can criminals hold your computer for "ransom"?

In May 2017, a dangerous new piece of malware, dubbed WannaCry, infected computers in 150 countries, rendering thousands of computers unusable and causing an estimated $4 billion in damage.[2] Britain's National Health Service was crippled, stopping many vital surgeries.[3] Say hello to ransomware, a new kind of "malware," or dangerous software that can infect computers and harm people.

Ransomware

Ransomware like WannaCry is a piece of software that invades your computer, locks up your files, and threatens to throw away the key unless you pay the criminals behind the operation.[4]

First, a malicious piece of software lands on your computer, often via an email attachment[5] or dangerous download.[6] This malware often exploits a flaw in an operating system that lets an attacker run whatever code they want on your computer.[7] WannaCry, for instance, exploited a bug in Microsoft Windows (interestingly, this bug was first discovered by the National Security Agency).[8] It's as if the people who built your house made a mistake on one of the locks, which would let a thief with a lockpicking set break in.

Once the malware is on your computer, it runs a program that encrypts all of your personal files. Encryption jumbles up the contents of files so people and apps can't understand them. But every encryption comes with a special passcode to undo the encryption, so you can un-jumble your files if you have this "key."[9] For instance, we could encode the message *"Meet me on the lawn"* to *"Zrrg zr ba gur ynja."* That wouldn't make any sense, of course, unless we told you that the way to decrypt it is to move all the letters 13 spaces down (so *a* becomes *n*, *b* becomes *o*, *c* becomes *p*, and so on). Once you did that to the encrypted text, you'd get back to *"Meet me on the lawn."*

So ransomware encrypts all of your files but refuses to tell you the key. The hackers say that, if you pay them, they'll give you the key and a program which will decrypt all your files. If you don't, they threaten to throw away the key forever, meaning your files will all be lost.[10]

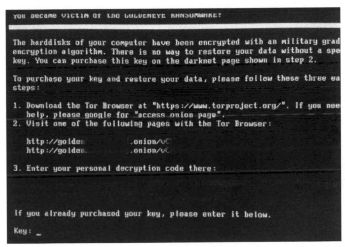

The screen shown to victims of a piece of ransomware called GoldenEye. Source: Wikimedia[11]

How do ransomers want you to send them money? You can't write them a check or Venmo them, because then people would know who they are and the government could crack down on them. Instead, ransomers demand payment through the anonymous online currency called Bitcoin.[12] Bitcoin is like an anonymous version of the money-sending app Venmo: anyone can send money to anyone else, but people are identified by anonymous codes called "Bitcoin addresses" instead of usernames.[13]

To unlock your computer, you'd need to visit a Bitcoin exchange website, which lets you convert dollars (or any "normal" currency) to Bitcoin and back, just like you could convert between dollars and pesos at a bank.[14] There's an "exchange rate" between Bitcoin and normal currency, just as there is between dollars and pesos, though this exchange rate is very prone to fluctuations.[15] The ransom for WannaCry was $300 in Bitcoin.[16]

You'd then use a specialized app called a "wallet" (analogous to Venmo) to send coins to the scammers. Then, the criminals promise, they will give you the key to unlock your files, and you'd be back on your way.[17]

If you're ever the unfortunate victim of a ransomware scam, we encourage you to not pay the ransom. If you do pay the ransom, you could be funding a vast online criminal enterprise[18] or hostile governments. For instance, the NSA linked the WannaCry attack to the North Korean government.[19]

The criminals get professional

The economics of ransomware make for some very strange occurrences. Since the scammers are anonymous and take your money *before* decrypting your files, they could in theory just take your money and run without giving you the decryption key.

However, the major ransomware attackers tend to actually give you the key. Why? Because the hackers realize that the only way they'll make money is if people keep forking over the ransom money. And people will only pay the ransom if they can trust that the scammers will decrypt their files.[20]

This has, strangely, led to scammers having excellent customer support, even sometimes having call centers and online chats with sales representatives.[21] Some even hire designers to make their websites look attractive.[22] They know that they need to build up a reputation of "trust" with their victims[23] — even though trust is a strange word to associate with someone who is extorting you and threatening to ruin your livelihood.

Who's at risk

Big organizations like businesses, hospitals, and governments are especially juicy targets for ransomers,[24] mostly because their IT departments are often slow to update old software and operating systems. Older operating systems are generally more at risk because they get fewer updates.[25]

To fight this problem, Microsoft usually quickly releases security updates to stop the malware; in WannaCry's case, Microsoft found the Windows bug that enabled the malware and offered it for free to users.[26] This patch was optional, but Microsoft forces some critical security updates on Windows users, whether or not IT administrators want it.[27]

Other tools that big organizations can use to fight back against malware include regularly backing up files to the cloud[28] (so ransomers can't paralyze them by encrypting files)[29] and antivirus software that regularly scans downloaded files for malware.[30] The best defense, though, is to be proactive.

Some organizations have started ditching traditional operating systems entirely, since they have huge "attack surfaces" — there are many places where malware can sneak in, such as via downloaded files and installed apps.[31] Google's ChromeOS, which powers Chromebooks, has become especially popular for the security-conscious because it is literally just a web browser; there are no conventional installable apps (which are a major entry point for malware). Plus, each Chrome tab runs in a "sandbox," meaning that the contents of a webpage can't touch any other parts of the computer.[32] But Chromebooks still have security holes like malware-loaded add-ons, and scams like phishing will never go away.[33]

How do people sell drugs and stolen credit card numbers online?

In 2013, the American government took down a website called Silk Road,[34] a sort of Amazon for the illegal: it sold drugs, fake passports, guns, hitmen, and the like.[35] Over two years, the website sold over $1 billion in contraband, and only a few of its buyers and sellers were caught.[36] Unfortunately, that wasn't the end; illegal online marketplaces have spread like wildfire ever since.[37]

How do these illicit markets work? How do people buy and sell on them? And why can't authorities put an end to them? Let's take a look.

Deep and dark web

As you can imagine, Silk Road and its successor sites can't work exactly like Amazon: if someone attached their name to every illegal transaction they did, it would be far too easy for the cops to find them. Instead, every buyer and seller on these sites is anonymous.[38] But that's not enough: the unique IP address of someone's computer could also be enough to identify them. So, to ensure total anonymity, Silk Road had to scramble all communication between users and the website.[39]

The "normal" internet that we browse every day doesn't work like that. Instead, Silk Road and other illegal marketplaces have had to turn to a pair of related concepts, the "deep web" and "dark web."[40]

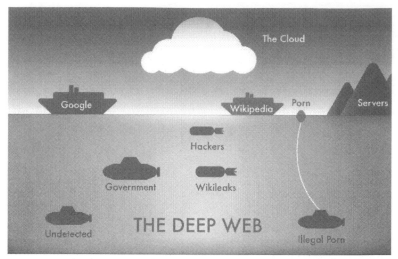

A schematic of the deep web. Source: ApploidWiz[41]

We'll start with the deep web. The deep web includes all the information on the internet that you can't find through a Google search. You can sometimes access these pages if another page sends you there. For instance, you can see your friends' Facebook posts, but those won't appear as search results.[42] Neither will many Google Drive files, medical records, legal documents, and so on.[43] Some people estimate that the deep web is 500 times larger than the "clear" web that we can find through Google.[44]

The deep web by itself isn't the key innovation behind the Silk Road. For that, look at the dark web. The dark web is a subset of the deep web that you can't access without special software that encrypts all communications and anonymizes your IP address.[45] Dark websites have long, strange URLs that end in *.onion*, and they reject any visitor that isn't using the special software.[46] Illegal marketplaces like the Silk Road use dark websites so that all activity on the site is untraceable.[47] In fact, you can't even figure out where dark websites' servers are, making them very difficult to take down. However, programming errors can leak the servers' IP addresses — which, incidentally, is exactly what led to Silk Road's demise.[48]

Accessing the dark web with Tor

Anyone can visit the dark web (it's not illegal, although many things that happen there are). You just need a special encrypting and anonymizing piece of software called Tor, short for The Onion Router.[49] Normally, when your computer connects to a website, your computer broadcasts its identity and which website it wants to visit, which makes it easy to track what websites everyone is visiting.[50]

But Tor is different. We'll explain with an example. Imagine you live in Seattle and want to mail some potato chips to your friend William in Philadelphia. Normally, you'd write your return address and William's address on the package. Anyone who looks at the package could tell that you're trying to talk to William. But what if chips are outlawed (the horror!) and you don't want anyone to know that you're sending some to him?

You can use several boxes nested inside each other. The outermost box, which we'll call Box 1, is addressed from Seattle to Denver. Inside that is Box 2, addressed from Denver to Chicago. And inside that is Box 3, addressed from Chicago to William in Philadelphia. Your chips are inside Box 3. On Box 1, you write a note: "open this box and put Box 2 in the mail." On Box 2, you say to "open this box and put Box 3 in the mail."

So you drop your mega-package in the mail in Seattle. When the Denver post office gets it, they dutifully remove Box 1 and put Box 2 in the mail. Box 2 gets to the Chicago post office, which unwraps it and puts Box 3 in the mail. That box would reach William.

This setup is complicated, but it totally anonymizes your communication. None of the post offices know that you're trying to send something to William: Seattle thinks you're sending something to Denver, Denver thinks you're sending something to Chicago, and Chicago only knows that someone from Denver is sending something to William.

This is how Tor works: it wraps your communication in several layers of encryption and bounces it around many intermediate "relay" computers, each of which only knows the previous and next computers in the chain.[51] This way, it's nearly impossible for anyone to trace communication over Tor; even the NSA reportedly has trouble with it.[52]

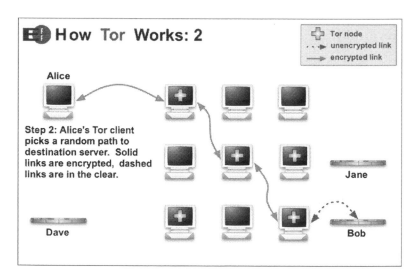

*Tor sends internet communications through several randomly-chosen
intermediate computers, making it nearly impossible to track which
websites you've visited. Source: Electronic Frontier Foundation[53]*

The nonprofit Tor Project offers a free browser called the Tor
Browser, a modified version of Mozilla Firefox, that uses this
technique.[54] So anyone who wants to hop on a dark website
can just download Tor and start browsing.[55]

How to browse (and take down) a dark market

To summarize, anyone who wants to visit a dark website needs
to start by downloading Tor. As we mentioned before, most
dark web URLs are intentionally hard to remember: the
investigative journalism nonprofit ProPublica has a dark
website hosted at propub3r6espa33w.onion.[56] (Yes, legitimate
websites use the dark web too!!)

Because it's so hard to remember dark web URLs, and because
there is (by definition) no search engine for the dark web,
people browsing the dark web start their search at a website
called The Hidden Wiki. (Technically, there are many
competing websites with this name, and no official one.) The
Hidden Wiki contains pages of dark web URLs so people can
find the sites they need.[57]

Once a visitor makes it to a dark market like the Silk Road, the
experience isn't much different than Amazon (besides the stuff
on sale, obviously): sellers have profiles, products have images,
previous buyers leave reviews.[58]

To preserve anonymity, all sales on dark markets are in anonymous currencies like Bitcoin. Buying something off a dark market isn't as simple as a direct payment. Instead, buyers send money to a centralized "escrow" account, which holds the money until the buyer confirms they've received the goods, at which point the money is released to the seller.[59]

Notice that transactions could only occur through the website, and at any given time a sizable amount of money was held in escrow. That centralization turned out to be the Silk Road's Achilles' heel.[60] Some programming mistakes by the Silk Road creator helped Feds find the physical location of Silk Road servers, which they seized in 2013. Since these servers contained all the code behind the Silk Road website and data for the Bitcoins in escrow, the Silk Road was immediately killed — a huge win for authorities.[61]

Unfortunately, many copycat sites popped up, and trying to take them down has been a game of Whac-A-Mole.[62] A spin-off site called Silk Road 2 popped up right after Silk Road went down. After it too was taken down in 2014, yet another market called AlphaBay appeared. AlphaBay was seized in July 2017,[63] but security experts fear that an even more dangerous black market — one immune to seizure — could be brewing.

An invincible black market?

Meet OpenBazaar, an online marketplace that joined the dark web in 2017.[64] Unlike the Silk Road, which had a central server (and, hence, an Achilles' heel), OpenBazaar is fully decentralized: every transaction happens directly between buyers and sellers. It's like going to a flea market instead of a supermarket. Flea markets are decentralized: shoppers and merchants exchange money directly. Supermarkets, on the other hand, are centralized: merchants sell their stuff to supermarkets, who then distribute items to shoppers. If you destroy the supermarket, no one can buy or sell anything. But the only way to take down a flea market is to take down every single vendor. If the Silk Road was like a supermarket, OpenBazaar is like a flea market.

Instead of connecting to a central website, every OpenBazaar user downloads some software that lets them talk to any other person using that software. When a buyer and seller find each other, they can agree on a price and trade directly.[65] Instead of having a centralized server to store Bitcoins in escrow, OpenBazaar lets buyers and sellers choose a third party to mediate disputes.[66]

In short, because OpenBazaar has no central authority, law enforcement can't take it down without seizing every single computer that runs the OpenBazaar software. So destroying OpenBazaar would be nearly impossible.[67] The founders of OpenBazaar say they won't police what's sold on the site[68] — in fact, given the distributed model, they probably couldn't police it anyway.[69] It's a radical idea, but a dangerous one.

Legitimate uses for the dark web

When you hear about all the crime on the dark web, it's easy to forget that there are legitimate uses for it. After all, the dark web is just a way to browse the internet anonymously.[70]

Several mainstream sites have started offering dark websites to protect their users. For instance, in 2014 Facebook made its website accessible over the dark web, which would make it accessible to political dissidents in countries where Facebook is restricted, such as China.[71] The whistleblowing nonprofit ProPublica also made a dark website in 2016 to help people avoid government censorship or tracking software that could target ads at them.[72]

Tor, the software used for accessing the dark web, is again nothing more than a privacy-enhancing web browser.[73] The Tor project names a wide list of people who can benefit from the anonymity of Tor:

> Individuals use Tor to keep websites from tracking them and their family members, or to connect to news sites, instant messaging services, or the like when these are blocked by their local Internet providers... Individuals also use Tor for socially sensitive communication: chat rooms and web forums for rape and abuse survivors, or people with illnesses... Journalists use Tor to communicate more safely with whistleblowers and dissidents.[74]

Finally, while Bitcoin is used a lot on the dark web, Bitcoin isn't part of the dark web — it's an independent technology with plenty of legitimate uses. Proponents argue that it protects buyers' and sellers' privacy[75] and that Bitcoin is less prone to political pressures since no government owns it.[76] But others fear that, if Bitcoin remains difficult for average users to learn, it will remain a tool primarily used by criminals.[77]

In short, none of these technologies — Bitcoin, Tor, the dark web — are illegal. Many illegal activities use these technologies, but we can use them for good too.

How does WhatsApp encrypt your messages so thoroughly that even WhatsApp can't read them?

Whether you're logging in to a website like Twitter, sending an email over Gmail, or buying something from Amazon, there are many situations when you'd want your communications to be encrypted so that eavesdroppers couldn't figure out your sensitive information.[78] For this, the web uses a technology called HTTPS, which automatically encrypts all information sent between your computer and a website's servers.[79]

Here's the catch, though: even though your information is encrypted between your computer and the server, the server can decrypt your information and read it.[80] Sometimes this is necessary: Amazon can't charge your credit card unless it can decrypt and read your credit card number. But sometimes companies use decrypted personal data in ways that upset customers. For instance, Google used to read your Gmail emails to target ads at you — at least until 2017, when the company backed down.[81] Another danger is that, if companies can decrypt your information, governments could coerce them to hand it over.[82]

So the messaging app WhatsApp was widely praised when, in 2014, it launched "end-to-end encryption," which only lets you and your recipient decrypt your messages. Neither WhatsApp nor its parent company, Facebook, can figure out what you're saying![83] Privacy advocates were thrilled by the move.[84] But how exactly can WhatsApp encrypt messages so well?

You've got (encrypted) mail

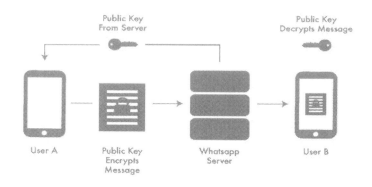

Public Key
From Server

Public Key
Decrypts Message

User A

Public Key
Encrypts
Message

Whatsapp
Server

User B

How end-to-end encryption works in WhatsApp. Source: Wired[85]

To explain end-to-end encryption, let's use an analogy. Suppose that in a particular country the postal service is evil and tries to open any package that's sent through the mail. Understandably, citizens are upset, but if they want to send things long distances, they have no choice but the postal service. So citizens devise a clever way to ensure that no one besides the intended recipient of a package, not even the postal service, can open the package.

Each person creates a key and hundreds of locks that can only be opened using that key. Everyone keeps their key in a secure place in their house, but they distribute their locks to hardware stores like the Home Depot around the country.

Say you live in this country and want to send a box to your friend Maria. You grab one of Maria's locks from your local hardware store and attach it to your box. When you mail the box to her, the postal service intercepts it. Of course, without the key, they can't open it! But when Maria gets the box, she can open it because she has the sole key that can open her lock.

This system is secure, since only the intended recipient can open the box. It's also clever because anyone can send stuff to anyone else without having to coordinate ahead of time. You just need to grab someone's lock from the store whenever you want to send them something.

This is also how end-to-end encryption works; the method is called "asymmetric encryption" or "public key cryptography."[86] With this method, every user is given a "public key" (which, in our example, is a lock) and a "private key" (which, in our example, is literally a private key). Every message is encrypted using the recipient's public key and can only be decrypted using their private key and some math.[87] All the encryption and decryption is done on users' devices, so it's completely impossible for the WhatsApp team to decrypt messages.[88]

A double-edged sword

End-to-end encryption is a victory for anyone who values privacy.[89] Journalists are particularly interested in end-to-end encryption, since they need more secure ways to communicate with sources given the rise in political censorship.[90] Political dissidents in repressive regimes like Syria have also started using end-to-end encrypted messaging apps like WhatsApp to get around government snooping.[91]

Unfortunately, the added privacy can also help terrorists, such as the ones who used encrypted messaging apps like WhatsApp to plan the 2015 Paris attacks.[92] Without text messages, a key piece of evidence, law enforcement has a harder time convicting criminals like these.[93]

What's more, WhatsApp's end-to-end encryption was blamed for a spate of brutal mob killings in India in 2018, which were sparked by fake news and rumors spreading like wildfire on WhatsApp. Because only the sender and receiver can understand end-to-end encrypted messages, WhatsApp messages are impossible to trace or stop, which left Facebook and the Indian police helpless to stop these fake news messages or even figure out who was sending them.[94] (Facebook has added features to WhatsApp to fact-check rumors[95] and restrict message forwarding,[96] but police will still never know where these messages came from.)

One thing's for sure, though. For better or for worse, end-to-end encryption is here to stay.

Why did the FBI sue Apple to hack the iPhone?

In 2016, the FBI asked Apple to help it unlock an iPhone used by one of the shooters in the deadly San Bernardino, California attack.[97] Apple had helped the government unlock iPhones over 70 times between 2008 and 2016,[98] but this time Apple refused, so the FBI sued them.[99] Why did all this legal drama happen? In a word: encryption.

Before this incident, Apple had just bypassed the password lock and handed the iPhones' files over to the Feds.[100] All 70 of those phones were running older versions of iOS, no newer than version 7, but the San Bernardino phone was on iOS 9.[101] The problem? In iOS 8, Apple removed the forced-bypass feature, making iPhones so secure that even Apple couldn't get in.[102]

Since iOS 8, an iPhone doesn't just check that the password you entered matches the stored password. It mashes up the password you enter with a 256-bit code (called a UID) that's unique to the phone and only stored on a secure place in the phone. Then your phone compares your mashup with the master mashup it has on file. This mashup, or "hash," can't be reverse-engineered, so there's no way to get in without knowing the stored password.[103]

If, like the FBI, you don't know the password to a phone, your only option is to randomly guess passwords, also known as brute forcing.[104] But Apple made this very hard too. Because you can't extract the UID from the phone, so the only way to try out passwords is the old-fashioned way — typing passwords in at the lock screen.[105] The nail in the coffin is that iPhones will wipe themselves clean after ten failed login attempts.[106]

That put the Feds in a jam. There was no way to get into the phone without randomly guessing passwords, and even then they'd only have ten tries.[107] They couldn't get Apple to disable the UID technology — that'd be physically impossible. But the FBI found a loophole: they pushed Apple to create a crippled version of iOS that didn't have the ten-try limit and would let the FBI enter passwords through a computer program instead of manually typing them in, which would speed up the brute-force testing.[108] Apple refused, saying that being forced to write code would violate the company's free-speech rights.[109]

A fierce legal battle ensued.[110] The tech community feared that an FBI victory would set a dangerous precedent of letting the government seize whatever encrypted data it wanted.[111] The FBI, of course, wanted the evidence.

The legal battle was never resolved because the FBI somehow managed to break into the shooter's iPhone without Apple's help.[112] To this day, we still don't know how the FBI broke in — despite several lawsuits demanding an explanation, the government continues to say it's a secret.[113]

The coda to this story is that the relationship between law enforcement and security gets more and more thorny every year. When the iPhone X introduced facial recognition for unlocking phones, many worried that police could just hold a phone up to a suspect's face and unlock it instantly — undermining the security of the whole system.[114]

How could a phony Wi-Fi network help someone steal your identity?

You walk into a Starbucks and turn on your Wi-Fi to bang out some emails. There are a couple open networks around called "Free Wi-Fi by Starbucks," "Google Starbucks," or "Free Public Wi-Fi." Which one do you connect to? (Choose one before you read on!)

Well, only "Google Starbucks" is a legitimate Wi-Fi network run by Starbucks.[115] If you chose one of the other two, you might be in trouble. Hackers often set up phony Wi-Fi networks designed to look like legitimate networks and try to dupe people into connecting to them.[116] If you connect to a hacker's network, that hacker's route sits between you and every website you want to connect to, so it can read every bit of information being sent back and forth.[117]

More sophisticated hackers realize that your computer broadcasts the names of networks it's connected to before, and it will automatically connect to any network with a name it remembers. So a hacker could read your device's network list and make their router spoof the name of a network your device remembers — and boom, your device will automatically connect to the phony router.[118] This way, a hacker could get you on their malicious Wi-Fi network without you doing anything!

Once you're on the hacker's Wi-Fi network, they can see and manipulate every message you exchange with websites and apps.

Bypassing HTTPS

Hold on, you might be thinking. *Doesn't HTTPS encrypt all communications?* That's true. If your connection uses HTTPS, the hacker won't be able to understand any information you're sending, and you'll be safe.[119] But there's a catch.

In 2009, a researcher released a tool called SSLStrip,[120] which lets an attacker fool your computer into talking with a server over HTTP instead of HTTPS.[121] You wouldn't notice a difference unless you looked at your address bar and realized there was no green padlock and no "https." Fortunately, web browsers have gotten pretty good at alerting users when they suspect an SSLStrip attack: they'll often cross out the "https://" in the address bar with a bright red slash, and they might show you an error like "This is probably not the site you are looking for!"[122]

But what if a hacker used SSLStrip and you didn't notice? You'd be connecting to websites and apps using HTTP instead of HTTPS. To see what's so dangerous about that, let's use an example.

Man in the middle

Suppose a woman named Sarah does online banking with Bank of America. Whenever she logs in, her browser sends her username and password to https://bankofamerica.com. This message could be *"Hi, I'm SarahTheGreat and my password is OpenSesame."* Since bankofamerica.com is served using HTTPS — the secure, encrypted method of connecting to websites — this message gets encrypted, or scrambled, before it's sent. Only Bank of America would be able to decrypt it and figure out Sarah's username and password. If a hacker gets his hands on Sarah's message to Bank of America, it would be gibberish, like *"Uv, V'z FnenuGurTerng naq zl cnffjbeq vf BcraFrfnzr."*[123]

But now suppose that Sarah goes to Starbucks and connects to the hacker's phony Wi-Fi. She opens up https://bankofamerica.com. But the hacker's router is using SSLStrip, and the router gives her http://bankofamerica.com instead. (Notice the difference? It's sent over HTTP instead of HTTPS!) One letter might not seem like a big deal, but because Sarah's only using HTTP now, her communication with bankofamerica.com isn't encrypted.[124] So when she logs in and sends the message *"Hi, I'm SarahTheGreat and my password is OpenSesame,"* the hacker's router can see that message in plain text — it isn't encrypted![125] The hacker could pass that information to bankofamerica.com, which wouldn't notice the difference; the hacker sent the right username and password, so it lets the hacker in.[126]

This is what's called a "man-in-the-middle" attack.[127] Once the hacker made Sarah communicate over unencrypted HTTPS, he could sit in the *middle* of Sarah and Bank of America and "hear" everything they were saying to each other. By getting Sarah's unencrypted password, the hacker could log into Sarah's account himself and, say, send funds to his account!

It's not just a danger with banking, though. With man-in-the-middle attacks, hackers could impersonate you to e-commerce sites, email, social networks, and the like — which could be devastating.[128]

Hackers using man-in-the-middle attacks aren't always out to just make a buck. In one famous case in 2013, the National Security Agency (NSA), which has long been criticized for spying on citizens, allegedly used a man-in-the-middle attack to impersonate google.com and spy on anyone who visited their impersonated page.[129]

Stay safe: use a VPN

Man-in-the-middle attacks succeed because of the innate insecurity of public Wi-Fi networks.[130] To protect yourself, experts recommend using a VPN, or virtual private network. VPNs create a sort of end-to-end encryption between you and the websites you're visiting, so your router can't harm you.[131] Technologists often say that VPNs create a direct, secure "tunnel" between you and websites.[132] Simply put, VPNs let you effectively turn a public Wi-Fi network into a private one.[133]

There are plenty of free or cheap VPNs out there.[134] We encourage using VPNs whenever you're on a public Wi-Fi network!

To summarize, how could a phony Wi-Fi network help someone steal your identity? Well, if a hacker got you to connect to their network and used SSLStrip, they could do a man-in-the-middle attack to get your passwords and other identifying information. That way, they could steal your identity without you ever knowing. As we mentioned in this last section, the best way to fight back against these man-in-the-middle attacks is to use a VPN.

Chapter 8.
Hardware & Robots

Throughout this book, we've focused on software. But even the fanciest apps are useless without hardware to run them on: phones, tablets, computers, watches, glasses, you name it. These devices have become quite powerful themselves: phones can replace credit cards,[1] sunglasses can record video,[2] and robots can fight wars without human intervention.[3]

So how do these silicon-based wonders work? Let's jump in.

What are bytes, KB, MB, and GB?

Whether you're shopping for a 128GB iPhone, downloading an app that's 50MB, or editing a 15KB document, you've probably run into measures of how big digital things are all the time. But what do KB, MB, and GB actually mean?

First, let's start with the basics: how do you write down information? We English-speakers write down information using 26 letters and ten digits, stringing them together into words and numbers, respectively. Meanwhile, computers only have two letters — 0 and 1 — and store all kinds of information, from text to images to movies, using a series of 1's and 0's. Each 1 or 0 is called a bit. Bits are too small to be of much use on their own, so we usually measure data in bytes, which are groups of eight bits.[4] For instance, the number we'd call 166 is 10100110 in binary (that number is 8 bits, or 1 byte, large).

A byte is a unit to measure file size, like how a yard is a unit to measure football fields. For instance, the average photo is 3 to 7 million bytes,[5] the average Android or iOS app is 38 million bytes,[6] and high-definition movies can be up to 25 billion bytes.[7]

Since files can get so big, we have a variety of units to measure file storage, just like we have centimeters, meters, and kilometers for measuring distance. A kilobyte (KB) is a thousand bytes, a megabyte (MB) is a million bytes, and a gigabyte (GB) is a billion bytes.[8] So, to return to our examples, a photos is 3-7 MB, an app is 38 MB, and an HD movie is up to 25 GB.

Beyond the "standard" units of KB, MB, and GB, there are terabytes (a trillion bytes), petabytes (a quadrillion bytes), and the exotic exabytes (a quintillion bytes).[9] Sometimes these units are useful: for instance, total internet traffic in 2013 was 5 exabytes, which is a jaw-dropping 5 billion GB, or 5 quintillion bytes.[10]

What do CPU, RAM, and other computer and phone specs mean?

Whenever you buy a MacBook, Samsung Galaxy phone, or any other device, you'll be bombarded with "specs," or numbers that explain how powerful and fast your device will be.[11] Some specs are pretty simple, like when the iPhone 7 says it comes with 32GB of storage.[12] But some of them are positively mystifying: what's a "quad-core Intel Core i9" and "512GB onboard SSD" anyway?[13]

It's enough to make your head spin. We could write a whole book about these specs, but let's look at the most important ones. Every computing device (laptops, tablets, phones, smartwatches, etc. — anything with an interactive screen) has these same features.

CPU: The Central Processing Unit

We'll start with the "brains of the operation," the Central Processing Unit, or CPU.[14] The CPU is a small, square chip that runs all the computations that make your device work, such as deciding what to draw on the screen, connecting to the internet, or crunching numbers.

The inside of an Intel CPU chip. Source: Eric Gabal[15]

CPUs are made of several smaller sections, called "cores," each of which can run computations separately.[16] CPUs with more cores are faster and can do more tasks at once.[17] It's like how, if four people are shoveling snow off a driveway at once, they can finish the job four times faster than if one person was trying to do it alone. Generally, devices whose CPUs have more cores can run more computationally intensive tasks like video editing apps, graphics-heavy games, or number crunching.

CPUs also have a clock speed, which is the number of calculations per second they can carry out.[18] Clock speeds are usually measured in gigahertz (GHz), which is a billion calculations per second.[19] In theory, a higher clock speed means a faster CPU. But most people don't really use clock speed to compare CPUs anymore, largely because there are too many other factors that determine CPU speed and because you can't really compare clock speeds across different brands of CPUs.[20]

Comparing CPUs head-to-head is tough because there are so many different factors that affect speed and power. To get a rough estimate of how two CPUs stack up, use the series number: Intel's CPU chips have numbers like i3, i5, i7, and i9.[21] Generally, the higher-numbered chips, like the i9, are faster and more powerful than the lower-numbered chips, like the i3.[22]

So what's the best CPU? It depends on what you need. The more powerful your CPU, the more it costs and the faster your battery drains.[23] So if you're just browsing Facebook and sending emails, you don't need a mighty CPU, just like you don't need a Ferrari if all you do is drive to the grocery store and back.

Finally, we'll touch briefly on the two major types of CPU chips: ARM and Intel. Intel chips (also known as x86) have traditionally been more powerful, while ARM chips have been cheaper and used less battery. So, traditionally, computers have used Intel while phones have used ARM. However, with ARM performance steadily improving, the lines have started to blur:[24] some Chromebooks run ARM while some run Intel, and Apple announced MacBooks would switch from Intel to ARM in 2020.[25]

Storage: long-term memory

Your device needs to store images, apps, documents, and other stuff you want to keep track of. For this, you need some form of long-term storage.[26] Let's start by looking at what's available on computers (that is, not phones or tablets — we'll talk about those in a bit).

The traditional way of storing digital data is the hard drive (HDD), which is a spinning metal plate coated with a layer of magnets that store your information. There's a special arm that reads and writes data to the drive.[27]

*A hard drive. Most hard drives are 2.5-3.5 inches in diameter.[28]
Source: Wikimedia[29]*

Then there's the newer solid-state drive (SSD), which has no moving parts but instead stores information in a huge grid of tiny boxes, called "cells."[30] Each tiny cell stores a 0 or 1.[31] (It's like how a waffle has a grid of squares on the surface, and you can pour syrup into individual squares if you want.) Since an SSD is little more than a bunch of cells, it has no moving parts. We'll get to why this is important in a bit. This technology is called "flash memory," and it's very common: SSDs, flash drives, and SD cards all use flash memory to store information.[32]

A solid-state drive. Notice there are no moving parts. Source: Wikimedia[33]

Hard drives vs. solid-state drives

So which form of storage is better? Hard drives are made of moving parts with fragile arms and discs,[34] so they break down faster (even with normal use), make noise, are heavy, and use lots of power.[35] Meanwhile, SSDs have no moving parts, so they're much sturdier, quieter, lighter, and more efficient.[36] Plus, hard drives need to spin around a moving disc to find information while SSDs just need to send pulses of electricity, making SSDs a good deal faster than hard drives.[37]

In other words, SSDs beat hard drives in almost every way: SSDs are lighter, quieter, sturdier, and more efficient.[38] Hard drives used to be cheaper per byte, but even that's going away as SSDs get cheaper every year.[39] A 1 TB SSD cost over $1000 in 2012 but is under $150 today — in fact, at this point, hard drives and SSDs are almost the same price per byte.[40]

So while hard drives were traditionally dominant in computers, SSDs are winning out. You can't even get MacBooks[41] or Microsoft Surfaces[42] with hard drives anymore; they all offer only SSDs.

Meanwhile, phones, tablets, and cameras can only ever use flash memory.[43] (Remember, SSDs are just a special kind of flash memory designed for laptops.[44]) One reason is that you can't even make a hard drive small enough to fit in today's mobile devices, since you can only shrink the spinning plates so much.[45] Therefore, smaller devices have had to use flash memory. Plus, flash memory is small, energy-efficient, and resistant to getting dropped, which are all very useful to have in mobile devices.[46]

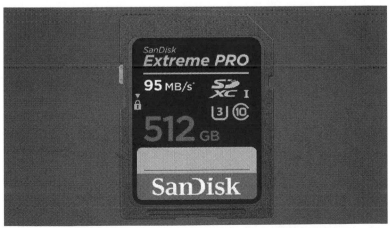

SD cards use flash memory, the same type of storage that phones and tablets use. Source: Mashable[47]

RAM: *short-term memory*

RAM, or random-access memory, is your device's short-term memory. (Humans have short-term memory too: it's what you use to temporarily remember a phone number as you're trying to type it in.[48]) Each app that you run, each browser tab you open, and each Word document you open consume some RAM as your computer tries to remember everything you're doing.[49] It's important to note just how fleeting RAM is. Whenever you restart an app, its RAM gets cleared. That's why, if you close a Word document without saving it, the contents will disappear. Similarly, whenever you restart your device, all your RAM is cleared. That's why your phone and computer have no running apps whenever you power them back on.[50]

Why do you need both RAM and storage? As an analogy, imagine you're doing some math homework on your desk and need to reference lots of notes and books. If you kept all your notes and books in your bookcase (which represents storage), you'd have to get up and walk over to the bookcase every time you wanted some information. That would be slow and inefficient. Instead, you could open all your books on your desk and sprawl out all your notes, which would make it easier for you to get all the information you need at a glance; this represents RAM. The caveat: the more stuff you put on your desk, the more cluttered and chaotic it gets, and eventually you'll just run out of room. That's like RAM: it helps your computer do many computations at once, but there's only a limited amount.[51]

What happens if you run out of RAM? (This might happen to you if you keep 2,000 tabs open.) Your computer will borrow some space (called "swap space"[52]) from your hard drive or

SSD and treat it like extra RAM, but this borrowed space takes much longer to access since storage is slower than RAM. As a result, your computer will run far more slowly.[53] That's why your computer crawls when you have a ton of apps, games, and tabs open. If this happens to you, you can close the memory-hogging apps to save RAM. Or you can just restart your device, which will wipe clean your RAM and let you start over.[54]

Overall, more RAM is better, though of course it costs more.[55] More RAM helps your computer handle heavy gaming, video editing, and apps that analyze lots of data. But if you're only going to be checking email or browsing the internet, you can get away with less RAM.[56]

More RAM will often make your computer faster, though it isn't a silver bullet because there could be other factors slowing you down, like the CPU.[57]

Tradeoffs

The big lesson to take away from this section is that hardware makers always need to make tradeoffs when designing devices. For instance, gaming laptops try to maximize RAM, but to keep costs down, they have to sacrifice battery life.[58] Some servers (the big computers that run websites) are specially designed to store images; they have more storage but sacrifice some RAM, since they won't be running many apps.[59] You can't have it all, so you'll have to figure out which features are the most important.

Why does Apple slow down old iPhones?

In 2017, Apple confirmed what many people had suspected for years: the company slows down older iPhones.[60]

Many people thought this was a moneymaking scheme from Apple — deliberately designing phones to break down quickly and thus forcing customers to buy new ones, a strategy called "planned obsolescence".[61] The reality, though, is a bit more mundane.

As phones age, their lithium-ion batteries get worse. Each time you charge your phone, that counts as a "charge cycle," and after 500 charge cycles iPhone lose about 20% of their original capacity.[62] (So if you've noticed that your battery life gets worse as your phone ages, you haven't gone crazy.) Meanwhile, since hardware is always improving, apps and iOS demand more and more energy and power as time goes on.[63]

That's a dangerous combination for your old phone: declining battery capacity and increasing demands for electricity. Your phone's battery life becomes awful, for one. And if apps ever demand more power than your phone's battery can provide, your phone might crash.[64]

To prevent random crashes, Apple decided to start slowing down older iPhones to reduce peak power usage, which would reduce the chance of crashes and improve battery life.[65]

Battery backlash

Consumers were, understandably, angry that Apple would intentionally slow their phones without telling them. Italy's antitrust agency, the AGCM, was upset that Apple steadily increased the demands on older iPhones (like by pushing newer and power-hungrier versions of iOS) without offering users a way to "recover the full function of their devices." The AGCM fined Apple 5 million euros for this offense.[66]

In response to the backlash, Apple announced that, for all of 2018, consumers could get their iPhone batteries replaced for $29 instead of the usual price of $79.[67]

This helped Apple's PR, but the program was just a little too good. Apple replaced 11 million batteries under the $29 program, far more than the 1-2 million they expected, and consumers noticed how much better their phones were after the replacement. In fact, their phones were so much better that many users didn't even bother upgrading to the iPhone XR and XS when they came out in late 2018.[68] The lack of upgrades, in turn, was a big reason why Apple CEO Tim Cook announced that revenues for the 2019 fiscal year would be $7 billion lower than previously expected.[69]

In short, the battery replacement program showed iPhone users that a simple battery change was enough to rejuvenate their phones, leading to fewer phone upgrades and a hit to Apple's earnings. The moral of the story: phones decay as they age, but not as much as you might think — and phone makers may not be eager for you to learn that.

How can you unlock your phone using your fingerprint?

As much as we love "swipe to unlock" lock screens on phones, we're excited about a new way of unlocking your phone: with your fingerprint. Since 2014, Samsung's Galaxy S phones have let you unlock the display using a fingerprint scanner.[70] The technology is popular in many other Android phones as well.[71] But how does it work?

Optical scanning

The oldest method of fingerprint scanning is "optical scanning," where a miniature camera literally takes a picture of your fingerprint. It edits the picture to make the "ridges" of your fingerprint black and the "valleys" white, generating a high-contrast version of your print. Then it compares that to an internal database of fingerprints to see if there's a match.[72]

The problem is that these scanners aren't very secure.[73] Since optical scanners just take a photo, you could fool a scanner by holding up a photo of a matching fingerprint; researchers even found one "master set" of prints that can trick 65% of optical fingerprint scanners.[74]

Capacitive scanning

These days, most people use a more secure method called "capacitive fingerprint scanning." Here, the sensor is covered with capacitors, or tiny batteries.[75] The raised ridges of your fingerprints increase the charge stored in the capacitors they touch, while the capacitors under the valleys of your fingerprints don't see a change in their capacitance. The phone uses the patterns of charge to build a high-resolution image of your print, and it checks the print against its database of prints as before.[76]

Proponents say that capacitive scanners are much more secure since you can't just fool them with a photo.[77] But one researcher hacked it anyway: he used a high-resolution image of his own thumb to make a plastic mold, which he used to fool his capacitive scanner.[78]

Biometrics

So even the best fingerprint scanning systems aren't entirely secure. That's why many phones have started offering more secure "biometric" login systems like iris recognition[79] and face recognition, which has been used on iPhones since the iPhone X launched in 2017.[80] And the Apple Watch reportedly considered identifying users based on their heartbeat patterns.[81]

Oh, before you get too comfortable, it's possible to hack these "more secure" biometric systems too. Remember the researcher who hacked a capacitive scanner using a fingerprint mold? He showed that he could also fool iris recognition hardware using high-resolution photos of his own eyes.[82] That just goes to show: no biometric identification system is perfect.[83]

How does Apple Pay work?

Since 2014, you've been able to pay for food, clothes, and other items in stores just by tapping your iPhone to a reader at the checkout line, a technology called Apple Pay.[84] Google followed suit with a similar service, Android Pay, in 2015.[85] How does this "magical" tap-and-pay system work?

Apple Pay in action. Source: Wikimedia[86]

Both Apple Pay and Android Pay are built off a technology called NFC, or Near-Field Communication.[87] With NFC, two devices (whether phones, cards, or payment terminals) containing a particular chip can exchange small amounts of information when touched together.[88] The devices exchange information using radio waves (incidentally, the same waves that Bluetooth uses).[89] NFC requires very little energy; some "passive" chip-holding devices don't even need any power to operate.[90]

Your phone has an NFC chip embedded in it, as does an Apple Pay payment terminal. When you tap your phone against the terminal, the two chips exchange information using radio waves. The terminal charges your credit card, and you've just bought your item.[91]

Another example of NFC: say you have a card that you use to pay for a subway or bus ride around town. The card contains a "passive" NFC chip that needs no power to operate. You touch the card to a reader, which contains an "active" chip that requires power, and the chips communicate. The reader subtracts the fare from your account balance (which the transit authority keeps on its servers) and opens the gates to let you in.[92]

Chicago's NFC-powered Ventra card, which you can use to pay for the subway. Source: Wikimedia[93]

Strengthened security

So how does Apple Pay keep you safe? Don't worry, your phone doesn't just send your credit card number to the store when you're using Apple Pay. Instead, Apple has worked closely with credit card vendors to make an extremely secure system. Whenever you use Apple Pay, the credit card vendor (like Visa or MasterCard) makes up a random 16-digit token that it associates with your card, encrypts the token, and sends it to your phone. When you tap on the terminal, your phone sends the encrypted token to the terminal. The terminal sends the token to the credit card vendor, who validates that it belongs to you and then charges you. This is a clever setup because, even if a hacker gets your token, there's no way to reverse-engineer your credit card number; only the credit card vendor could do that. Furthermore, on iPhones that have Touch ID, Apple makes you verify the payment with a fingerprint. As a result, commentators call Apple Pay "much safer" than credit cards.[94]

It's no surprise that stores are eager to start accepting Apple Pay, since it makes them immune from hackers who try to steal their credit card data[95] — such as when Target was hacked to the tune of 40 million credit card numbers in 2013.[96] This became even more important in 2016, when new laws made retailers (instead of card issuers) financially liable for any hacks that occur because of the old magnetic-swipe credit card reading technology.[97] Chip-based credit cards would also help retailers avoid hacks, but they're much slower than magnetic-swipe cards, making Apple Pay a more attractive alternative.[98]

Apple Pay is a win-win, so we imagine that Apple Pay and other NFC-based mobile payment systems will see even more uptake in the coming years.

Other uses for NFC

NFC is pretty simple — touch your phone to something to exchange money or information — but that simplicity makes it a powerful tool that might have many farther-reaching applications.

A first example: there are a huge variety of things you can start paying for using NFC. San Francisco has started letting you pay for parking meters by tapping your phone against an NFC sticker.[99] And Chicago has started letting you use Apple Pay to pay for the subway.[100]

Furthermore, with NFC, you can tap your phone against anything with a special sticker to get more information about it. Marketers could embed NFC stickers into advertisements or flyers, and people could just tap their phone against the stickers to learn more. In certain French cities, you can tap your phone against NFC stickers to get maps of the area. And NFC could also help in retail shopping: tap your phone against a package to comparison shop or find coupons, for instance.[101] NFC is helping blur the line between the physical and digital world, and we think the uses of NFC will get more and more exciting.

How does Pokémon Go work?

The mobile game Pokémon Go took the world by storm in 2016 by letting you find Pokémon, those virtual cartoon monsters, just by walking around the real world.[102] One of the most popular features of Pokémon Go was how it overlaid the world of Pokémon on top of your world, a technique called augmented reality (AR).[103] For instance, you could see PokéStops (places to find items) and Pokémon Gyms (places to battle other Pokémon) at real landmarks around your town.[104] You also find Pokémon in their "natural habitats": water-typed Squirtles on the beach, for instance, or bat-like Zubats at night.[105] It's thanks to a mashup of crowdsourced location information, your phone's internal clock, and some geographic data that classifies an area based on its "climate, vegetation, and soil or rock type."[106]

The more technically interesting part is where you can see a Pokémon overlaid on your immediate environment while trying to capture them. For instance, if you're trying to catch a Pokémon in a park, it could be "jumping" around on the grass or splashing in a fountain.[107]

How does your phone know where to put the Pokémon? First, it uses your camera to get a sense of the immediate environment, such as a grassy area by a river. Pokémon Go then uses some algorithms to figure out where the ground is and draws the Pokémon standing there.[108] Then it uses your accelerometer, compass, and GPS to notice if you're moving around, in which case the game moves and rotates the Pokémon appropriately.[109]

It's an exciting time for augmented reality, in no small part because of Pokémon Go. In 2016, one expert predicted that AR would be a $90 billion market by 2020.[110] Game developers are especially excited.[111] But for now, at least, go catch 'em all.

How does Amazon manage to offer 1-hour delivery?

Amazon's Prime Now, an add-on to their Prime subscription service, lets you get a huge range of items delivered to your door in an hour or less[112] in over 30 cities across the US, as of 2017.[113] But flying cross-country takes at least 5 hours[114] — so how on earth could Amazon pull off 1-hour delivery?

Amazon uses a combination of software, robots, and humans to pull this off. First, the software: Amazon uses data about its Prime subscribers in an area to decide what items to store in warehouses in the area, a move designed to optimize the speed of deliveries.[115]

The center of the action is Amazon's warehouses, which it calls fulfillment centers, located right outside the major metro areas that Prime Now serves. For instance, there's one in Union, NJ, right outside New York City.[116]

Inside, products from granola bars to skateboard shoes are stacked on shelves scattered around the warehouse floor. A fleet of hockey puck-shaped robots move around the warehouse to find shelves containing the proper product and move them toward a human employee, called a "picker," who grabs the item from the shelf.[117]

While products in most stores are sorted thematically (with, say, all the breakfast foods in one aisle), items in the Amazon warehouses are scattered randomly (with, say, potato chips next to a board game). This way, the robots will never be too far from any particular item.[118] Plus, human workers restocking shelves don't have to worry about where they put items.[119]

Human workers would never be able to track down a particular item, but that's okay because Amazon's huge databases keep track of exactly where each item is. Amazon's algorithms also control what items go where, what routes the robots take, and what routes employees take around the warehouse.[120]

Amazon claims that the robots and algorithms can help Amazon retrieve a customer's items in just a few minutes, instead of the hours it'd take otherwise.[121]

Once the items are in bags, Amazon hands them off to a team of "couriers," people who use any means necessary — subway, car, bike, or foot — to get the item to the customer before the hour is up.[122]

This case is an interesting look into the future of the workplace, where humans and robots will cooperate. Robots can find and move items around much faster than humans can, especially since these robots can tap into algorithms to minimize their travel time. But humans have the uniquely nimble fingers needed to grab items out of the shelves, scan them, and put them in bags.[123]

What does that mean for jobs? It's a little paradoxical. E-commerce is eliminating thousands of retail jobs, but Amazon's robots and algorithms make rapid fulfillment centers possible, and that ends up *creating* jobs.[124] Perhaps the best example of this paradox: technology and automation have killed thousands of jobs in the Rust Belt town of Joliet, Illinois, but Amazon brought 2,000 jobs back when it opened a fulfillment center there in 2016.[125]

So if you ever need to get something urgently and rely on Prime Now, be sure to thank the people — and robots — who made it happen. It's an interesting collaboration.

How could Amazon deliver items in half an hour?

Think one-hour delivery was impressive? Amazon won't stop there. They want half-hour deliveries using drones. But how?

Amazon's idea for this service, called Amazon Prime Air, is to start the packaging process the same way as in the one-hour case but replace human deliverers with drones — or "unmanned aerial vehicles," as Amazon calls them.[126]

At the warehouse, Amazon would strap a package to a drone. The drone would fly to the recipient's house and either drop the package via parachute or land on a specially marked pad. And it would do so without any human control.[127]

An Amazon drone delivering a package. Source: Amazon[128]

So, is this coming soon? We wish. Amazon still needs to teach its drones how to manage bad weather and avoid buildings and other drones.[129] Another issue is that Amazon only has drone fulfillment centers in 24 American states, most of which are along the coasts.[130]

But the biggest issue is regulation; the Federal Aviation Administration (FAA) has proven to be a thorn in Amazon's side. One regulation says that drones can't fly within 5 miles of an airport, which blocks most of New York City.[131] Another policy issued in 2015 said that autonomous drones couldn't fly outside the operator's field of vision, which would prevent drones from flying autonomously.[132] Amazon has been trying to push the FAA to loosen these regulations; they scored a win when the FAA dropped the field-of-vision rule in 2016[133] — probably in large part due to Amazon's pressure. (It shocks us sometimes that tech companies have so much power over policymakers.)

Still, Amazon is still frustrated by the FAA's regulations. Amazon is so annoyed, in fact, that they opened up a drone testing center in Canada just 2,000 feet from the American border.[134] And because the FAA hasn't been helpful, Amazon has done most of their drone testing in the United Kingdom.[135] In fact, the first successful Amazon drone delivery took place in Cambridgeshire, England in December 2016.[136]

Amazon's delivery drone up close. Source: Amazon[137]

While it might seem weird to imagine delivery drones buzzing around in the air, Amazon envisions that, one day, they'll be a perfectly normal sight.[138] Eventually, these drones might even become as common as FedEx or UPS trucks.

In conclusion, let's back up and get some perspective. Imagine if you went back in time to 50 years ago and told people that you owned a handheld computer (i.e. a phone), wirelessly bought an item with that computer, and got that item delivered to you by a flying robot with wings. They'd think you're crazy. But, as you now know, it's real, and it's really exciting.

Chapter 9.
Business Motives

One of the greatest understatements of the 21st century is that tech has come to dominate the business world. Apple, Amazon, Facebook, Microsoft, and Google's parent company Alphabet all routinely top the list of the world's most valuable companies.[1]

But having a great app isn't enough. The startup graveyard is littered with the skeletons of startups that had popular apps but didn't understand fundamental business principles — look no further than MoviePass, which offered unlimited movies for $10 a month but flamed out spectacularly in 2018 because it had a poor business model.[2]

Meanwhile, traditionally non-technology companies, from supermarkets[3] to banks[4] to restaurants,[5] have had to start building apps to avoid falling behind. As Salesforce cofounder Parker Harris put it: "all business leaders need to be technologists... and every enterprise needs to become an app company."[6]

So why do tech companies make the moves they make? And how do non-tech companies adapt to the digital age? Let's dive in.

Why does Nordstrom offer free Wi-Fi?

You've probably gotten used to free Wi-Fi at coffee shops like Starbucks, which has offered Wi-Fi to customers since 2010.[7] It makes sense why they offer it — people who want to get some work done flock to Starbucks.

In 2012, the retailer Nordstrom started offering free Wi-Fi in stores,[8] and other retailers like the Home Depot and even Family Dollar are jumping on the bandwagon too.[9] But why? No one goes to Nordstrom to fire off some emails. (If you do, we won't judge.) Do stores offer free Wi-Fi just to be nice?

It turns out that offering free Wi-Fi can help Nordstrom's profits quite a bit. To understand this, let's first break down how Wi-Fi works. When you turn on Wi-Fi on your phone, your phone sends out a radio signal to find nearby Wi-Fi hotspots (also called routers), which are those boxes with antennas that you might have in your house.[10] Hotspots let your phone connect to the internet. The radio signals your phone sends out include a unique code that's embedded in the phone, called the MAC address.[11] So, whenever you connect to a Wi-Fi hotspot, the hotspot's owner can see your MAC address.[12] If they keep your MAC address on file, they can remember you if you reconnect.

An example of a wireless hotspot, also known as a wireless router.
Source: Wikimedia[13]

In 2012, retailers like Nordstrom realized they could track which Wi-Fi hotspots shoppers were connected to and, using that information, pinpoint shoppers' locations.[14] But how?

The secret is a technique called triangulation, which, incidentally, is also how your GPS system knows where you are.[15] Triangulation starts when you're connected to three hotspots. Each hotspot will see your MAC Address and notice it's the same, so they'll all know it's you. Then each hotspot will measure the strength of the radio signal from your phone to the hotspot to calculate how far your phone is from the hotspot; the farther away you are, the weaker the radio signal.[16] Some software draws a circle around each hotspot, with the radius equaling your distance from the hotspot. The three circles will intersect in a single point, which is where you must be — and, voila, the software has triangulated your location! The owner of a company that uses triangulation says they can figure out someone's location within 10 feet.[17]

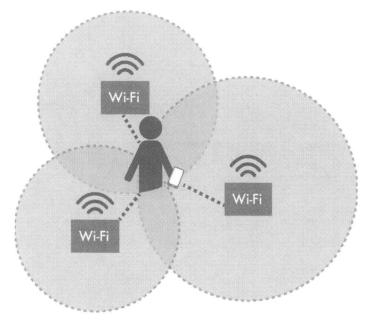

Wi-Fi triangulation, which lets Wi-Fi network owners pinpoint where a shopper is standing. Source: Skyhook[18]

With triangulation technology, retailers like Nordstrom can monitor shoppers' locations and movements throughout a store.[19] This can be pretty useful. For instance, if a store notices that most people walk straight through the hats department to get to the women's department, they could reduce their inventory of hats and stock up on women's clothing.[20] They can figure out which days and times are the busiest and adjust the number of salespeople or cashiers accordingly. One company even lets retailers measure how many people pause outside the storefront and then walk in — which helps the retailers figure out which window displays are the most effective.[21] This entire method is highly profitable.[22]

So, why do companies like Nordstrom offer free Wi-Fi? Offering Wi-Fi gets shoppers to turn on their phones' Wi-Fi connections, which makes them start shooting radio waves at Wi-Fi hotspots. The store can then use triangulation to track their movements. And that, as we've seen, means big bucks.

Digging up more data

When Nordstrom started using Wi-Fi triangulation software, they argued it was all anonymous, so it was no big deal. They would know your phone's MAC address, but that wasn't enough to figure out who you were.[23] (Think about it — do you even know your own phone's MAC address?)

But retailers have clever ways of figuring out who you are based on your MAC address. For instance, stores can make you sign in with your email address before you can use their free Wi-Fi, which lets them tie your MAC Address with your email address. Then, stores can link your in-store activity with your online activity. For instance, if you were browsing for scarves on macys.com, you could, in theory, get a coupon for scarves as soon as you walked into a Macy's store.[24]

Stores could make this data even more powerful by combining it with video surveillance. Some new video cameras installed in stores are reportedly so good that they can guess your age, gender, and ethnicity just from video footage.[25] They can also tell which specific products you looked at and how long you looked at them.[26] This information, combined with your in-store movement data and online purchase data, is juicy stuff for store owners.

Eventually, stores could even start sending you targeted coupons via push notifications if you start looking at a product but start walking away.[27] This would probably only work for shoppers connected to the store's Wi-Fi network — which is another reason to offer free Wi-Fi.

Love it or hate it?

Tracking customers with tools like Wi-Fi and video surveillance is clearly profitable for retailers, who are struggling with problems of "showrooming," where people browse for things in stores but eventually buy them online.[28] The more data stores get on users, the better positioned they are to make the sale.

But what about customers?

Well, on the plus side, this could help stores give you a better experience by getting rid of unpopular products or ensuring there are enough employees on the floor at any time.[29] If stores knew how often you came to shop, perhaps they could start offering loyalty programs that would help you out. And the targeted coupons could help you find a bargain.[30]

The downside is privacy. It's shocking how much information stores can learn about you; from your shopping habits to your physical appearance, they can literally track your every move.[31] The worst part about Nordstrom's case is that the retailer didn't tell their customers they were being tracked — and when people found out, they weren't happy.[32] To combat this problem, Nordstrom offered a way for customers to opt out of being tracked. But commentators complained that this scheme was opt-*out*, not opt-*in*, meaning customers who didn't know about the tracking would unwittingly be tracked.[33]

If you don't like the surveillance, we have bad news — it's tough to stop. Researchers found that some phones scan for Wi-Fi networks even if you have turned off Wi-Fi, meaning that you'd need to turn off your phone to stop the tracking. But some phones will still search for Wi-Fi networks even when they're off. You'd have to take your phone's battery out (or smash it with a hammer) to completely put a stop to this. But even then, you can't avoid video tracking.[34]

In response, retailers say that Wi-Fi tracking is no worse than shopping online, where e-retailers like Amazon can track your every click.[35] But privacy advocates would probably argue that tracking someone's clicks is much less creepy than tracking someone's physical movements.

So it's a mixed bag. But whatever you think of Nordstrom's free Wi-Fi, you've got to admit that it's a clever business move.

Why does Amazon offer free shipping with Prime membership even though it loses them money?

Since 2004, Amazon's Prime service has let you get free two-day shipping on millions of products[36] if you subscribe for $119 a year.[37] It's a huge program: two-thirds of all American households are on Prime.[38]

Shipping things quickly and freely across the globe isn't cheap, though. Amazon loses over $8 billion a year from its free 2-day shipping program.[39] If Prime loses them so much money, why does Amazon offer it?

Amazon's strategy

Before we explore some reasons, it's important to note that Amazon tends to care more about increasing revenue than increasing profits. That's because it's historically reinvested its revenue back into the company instead of giving it to shareholders.[40] This strategy helps Amazon grow its business as quickly as possible to maximize long-term growth.[41] And, in general, retail is a low-margin business.[42]

In other words, Amazon has intentionally taken in very little profit. For instance, in 2016 Amazon made $136 billion in revenue but took a puny $2.4 billion in profit.[43] That's actually far more profit than previous years, where their profit hung around zero; in 2012, Amazon actually lost $39 million[44] despite taking in $61 billion in sales.[45]

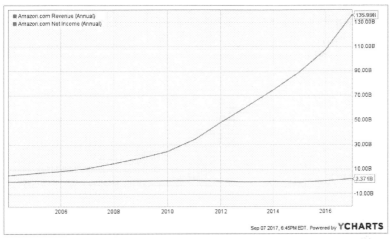

*Amazon's revenue (top line) is growing like crazy, but they've been intentionally keeping their profit (or "net income"; bottom line) low.
Source: YCharts*[46]

How Prime cashes in

So, Amazon's goal with Prime is probably to grow their revenue. Here a couple key ways Prime helps Amazon bring in more sales.

First, Prime is a powerful loyalty program that gets customers to spend more and more money on the platform. Prime's 100 million members are estimated to spend over twice as much money on Amazon per year as non-members.[47] Granted, part of this is because bigger spenders are more likely to join Prime in the first place. However, there are a few reasons why just joining Prime could get someone to spend more. One reason is that two-day shipping grants instant gratification (well, more instant than normal shipping), which enables "thoughtless" impulse buying.[48] A second reason could be that, once people commit the $119 a year for Prime, they feel the need to buy a lot of stuff (and get a lot of free shipping) to justify that spending.[49] Data seems to support this theory: one study found that loyalty programs increase sales by 20%.[50]

Second, Prime members do a greater proportion of their shopping on Amazon. Many Prime members default to shopping on Amazon even if the item they want to buy is cheaper somewhere else, perhaps because using Amazon has just become a habit.[51] Plus, it's hard to beat free two-day shipping, so many Prime members will buy from Amazon even if they originally found the item on another site.[52] The numbers are stunning: a Prime member who begins their search on Amazon is 12 times less likely to also visit Walmart.com than a non-Prime member.[53] In other words, Prime makes customers even more loyal.

Third, Prime started a race to the bottom, which hurts its competitors. Prime has conditioned customers to expect two-day shipping,[54] so Amazon's competitors are being forced to offer free two-day shipping just to stay competitive. There are plenty of examples. Target offered free shipping during the 2014 holiday season.[55] In 2017, Walmart started offering free two-day shipping on orders over $35.[56] And in 2010 a consortium including Toys "R" Us and Barnes & Noble even created a Prime clone called ShopRunner, which had the same benefits (free two-day shipping if you buy from any of the companies) and price point as Prime.[57] The spread of two-day shipping is great for consumers, but it could be a death sentence for retailers without the money or infrastructure to ship that much stuff that fast.[58]

Growing Prime

It's clear that Amazon wants more people to join Prime. So it's no surprise that Amazon keeps cramming as many features as possible into Prime. These days, Prime includes not only free shipping but also free movies, hundreds of thousands of free Kindle e-books, and music streaming.[59]Prime has grown so much that it's even entered the offline world: once Amazon bought Whole Foods in 2017,[60] Prime members started getting 10% off at Whole Foods stores, among other perks.[61]

Even though Prime might look like a losing proposition on the surface, it's a treasure trove for Amazon. Bloomberg even called it the "most ingenious and effective customer loyalty program in all of e-commerce, if not retail in general."[62]

Why does Uber need self-driving cars?

In 2015, Uber poached an entire team of robotics faculty from Carnegie Mellon University[63] and set up an office in Pittsburgh dedicated to self-driving cars.[64] Former Uber CEO Travis Kalanick said that developing an autonomous vehicle was "basically existential" for the company.[65] Why does Uber have such drive to self-drive?

The pitfalls of growth

The first thing you have to know is that Uber hasn't been in the best financial straits, losing over $1 billion a year. A big reason for that has been its continued insistence on growth over profits.[66] For years, Uber has fought tooth-and-nail to offer lower prices than Lyft, which has led to aggressive discounts[67] — so aggressive, in fact, that Uber actually loses money on most rides.[68]

Meanwhile, Uber has kept investing in expensive growth areas like food delivery and electric scooters — which is great for increasing revenue but bad at keeping costs down.[69] It also dumped large amounts of money into failed expansions into China,[70] Russia,[71] and Indonesia.[72]

In short, Uber's drive for growth has made it impossible to turn a profit — so it'll need to find a new way to radically cut costs if it wants to get out of the red. But where can Uber cut costs?

Driving problems

Uber's other big problem is with drivers. Driver retention is low — only 4% of people who sign up to drive for Uber are still driving a year later[73] — meaning that Uber has to offer boatloads of bonuses and incentives just to keep drivers around.[74] In the end, Uber only takes a roughly 20% cut of the profits on each ride,[75] presumably because it needs to pay the rest to drivers.

So Uber is stuck between a rock and a hard place: it has to slash prices to keep enough riders on the platform, and it has to increase payments to keep enough drivers on the platform. Without riders, nobody would drive, and without drivers, nobody would ride. In other words, Uber is a two-sided market — it has to match riders with drivers — and so it has to cater to both, slashing its margins on both ends.[76]

The self-driving solution

You can see the appeal of self-driving cars now. We think there are three big reasons why Uber is investing so heavily in self-driving cars.

First, Uber wouldn't have to deal with human drivers, which would let Uber pay out less per ride and not have to worry about driver retention (your robotic cars will, hopefully, never leave you). Sure, Uber would need to take on the costs of gas and maintenance of the cars (which are currently the drivers' responsibilities), but this pales in comparison to how much Uber would save by not having to pay drivers.[77] One study found that a self-driving fleet would cost just one-tenth as much to operate as a normal taxi fleet — something that would definitely help Uber move toward profitability.[78]

Second, riders would have strong reasons to prefer self-driving cars. Autonomous Ubers would be far cheaper for consumers[79] and, according to one expert, would cut accident rates by 90%.[80] So offering self-driving cars would help Uber attract customers and grow its user base.

Third, in order to stay competitive, Uber knows it has to develop self-driving cars before its competitors do.[81] There are a lot of players making big bets on self-driving cars: Google's self-driving car project Waymo has started collaborating with Lyft to create self-driving cars,[82] Ford invested $1 billion in a self-driving car startup called Argo AI, and Tesla has built the hardware needed for its cars to be autonomous.[83] Every company wants to be the first to master self-driving cars.[84] Because self-driving cars will be so much cheaper to operate, the first company to make them mainstream will get a significant edge,[85] and the winner will also be able to earn money by licensing its self-driving software to competitors.[86] In other words, Uber would rather make its own autonomous car instead of being forced to buy solutions from its rivals.

Why did Microsoft acquire LinkedIn?

In 2016, Microsoft bought the professional social network LinkedIn for a jaw-dropping $26.2 billion — Microsoft's largest acquisition to date, and the third-biggest tech acquisition in history at the time.[87] Why would the company behind Windows and productivity tools splurge so much on a social network?

Owning the enterprise

Microsoft's traditional moneymakers, Windows and devices, have long been on the decline.[88] Sales of PCs and Surface tablets shrank 26% from 2016 to 2017 alone.[89] Microsoft was never able to get a foothold in the massive mobile space; Windows Phone was a flop.[90]

Instead, Microsoft knows that its future (and present) is in enterprise software, or tools built for businesses; Azure (Microsoft's cloud computing platform aimed at businesses) and Office 365 are the company's most profitable and fastest-growing segments.[91] Nothing shows this pivot better than Microsoft CEO Satya Nadella's new mission for the company, unveiled in 2015: "to empower every person and every organization on the planet to achieve more." (It's quite a change from Bill Gates's old mission of putting "a computer on every desk and in every home.")[92]

The LinkedIn purchase was very important for Microsoft because it cemented the company's place as a leader in the enterprise space.[93] We think there are three big ways this purchase helped Microsoft solidify its dominance.

First, acquiring LinkedIn helps Microsoft become the center of the businessperson's world, much like Facebook or Instagram might be the center of your online social life.[94] Making a presentation with PowerPoint? You're using a Microsoft product. Taking a Windows laptop to a meeting? You're again using a Microsoft product. Looking up potential clients or employees? You're probably using LinkedIn, which is now a Microsoft product.

Because so much of business workers' work-related lives — emails, documents, professional profiles, and so on — use Microsoft products, Microsoft thinks it can make your LinkedIn profile your central professional "source of truth."[95]

With LinkedIn, Microsoft wanted to become the center of people's professional lives. Source: Microsoft SEC filing[96]

Second, by acquiring LinkedIn's 433 million users,[97] Microsoft got a huge data source — which it calls "the social graph"[98] — that can improve its existing enterprise offerings. That is, Microsoft could mix LinkedIn's data and profiles into tools like

Office apps. For example, your Outlook calendar could show the LinkedIn profile of the next person you're meeting with, and Cortana (Microsoft's version of Siri or Alexa) could give you tips on how to impress them. Salespeople using Microsoft's customer relationship management tool, Dynamics CRM, could use potential clients' LinkedIn profiles to have a better idea of how to pitch their product. Or, Office 365 could analyze a company's organization chart on LinkedIn to see what kinds of talent they need to add.[99] With this exclusive data, Microsoft can build features that set its products apart from competitors like Salesforce (a CRM system that competes with Microsoft's Dynamics)[100] or Google's G Suite (which offers Google Drive and Gmail to businesses).[101]

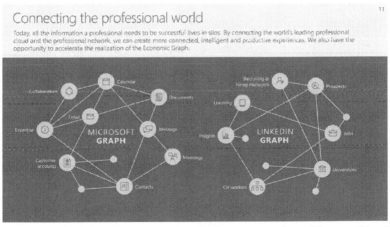

Microsoft wants to combine its data on business workers, like email and calendar, with LinkedIn's data, like workers' relationships with colleagues and their list of past jobs. They call the combined dataset the "Economic Graph." Source: Microsoft SEC filing[102]

The third reason was defensive: Microsoft wanted to keep LinkedIn's valuable data and gigantic user base away from potential competitors in the enterprise space. Salesforce made a major offer in stock for LinkedIn, but Microsoft countered with an all-cash offer (cash is usually more attractive than stock) and more potential synergies that would help LinkedIn grow.[103] By beefing up Dynamics CRM with LinkedIn's treasure trove of data, Microsoft was suddenly able to compete on even footing with Salesforce's top-notch CRM solution.[104] (Had Salesforce gotten LinkedIn, Microsoft would have been at an even greater disadvantage.)

Money and people

As we've seen, the LinkedIn purchase was designed to help Microsoft solidify its position in the business market. Besides that, there are two factors that always affect acquisitions: money and people.

In terms of money, LinkedIn pulled in a small profit ($71 million) a year before Microsoft acquired them,[105] which is always a welcome addition. LinkedIn has good revenue prospects because it has a nicely diversified revenue stream, split between premium subscriptions, advertising, and tools for recruiters.[106] Furthermore, LinkedIn continued to grow quickly after the acquisition, adding 70 million users (or 15%) within 10 months of being bought.[107] All of these are positive signs for further earnings for Microsoft.

People are extremely important as well. LinkedIn's chairman Reid Hoffman, who also founded PayPal and has worked on startups for over 20 years, is one of the best-connected and most-liked people around Silicon Valley.[108] When Hoffman joined Microsoft's board, he said he would help Microsoft build stronger connections around Silicon Valley[109] — a key asset for Microsoft, which for many years was unpopular in the Valley.[110]

So, in summary, why did Microsoft buy LinkedIn? There are many factors, but the underlying theme is that it helped Microsoft maintain its much-needed chokehold on the enterprise space and keep the valuable business and data of LinkedIn away from its opponents.

Why did Facebook buy Instagram?

In 2012, Facebook bought the hot photo-sharing social network Instagram for $1 billion.[111] But, at the time, Instagram had zero revenue and no plans to make revenue — so why would Facebook spend so much to buy them?[112]

It can be summed up with two words: *mobile photos.*

First, mobile. Facebook started as a desktop web company, but by 2012 they began to realize that the future was on mobile devices.[113] While half of Facebook's users logged in on a mobile device in 2012, Facebook hadn't figured out how to monetize mobile at all, and their mobile apps and website were accused of clutter and long page load times.[114] Facebook announced it wanted to be a mobile company, but it wasn't sure how to.[115]

Second, as mobile phones grew in popularity, taking and sharing photos became even easier, making photo sharing the next big thing in social media.[116] Facebook had been founded in the era of text-based status updates, and it showed.[117]

Enter Instagram, a hot new social network focused on mobile photos. It was an immediate hit; its Android app picked up a million users in the first day it was available.[118] Mobile users preferred Instagram's photo-sharing experience to Facebook's because Instagram was cleaner and photo-centric, plus it had filters.[119]Facebook recognized that Instagram was beating it at mobile photos[120] and feared that Instagram would become the primary way people shared photos with the world.[121]

So Facebook snapped up Instagram for $1 million to make sure it would dominate the future of mobile photos, even if its flagship app didn't.[122] Rumors had swirled that Google[123] and Twitter[124] wanted to buy Instagram, so it's little wonder that Facebook swooped in so decisively.

Recurring victories

Back in 2012, commenters were unsure if the Instagram acquisition was a smart move, with some calling it a sign of a "Web bubble."[125]

But ever since, Instagram has proved itself to be a worthwhile acquisition. It kept up its growth, expanding from 30 million users in 2012 to over a billion by 2018.[126] More notably, Facebook succeeded in bringing targeted ads to Instagram, a platform that originally had no monetization strategy; Instagram ads now pull in over $8 billion a year.[127]

Instagram also helped Facebook neutralize Snapchat, which had started threatening Facebook's growth, especially among teens, by 2016.[128] But in 2017, Instagram copied Snapchat's most famous feature, Stories,[129] which demolished Snapchat, slowing the app's growth by 82%.[130] Instagram had proved, yet again, why it was such a valuable asset for Facebook.

So it's no wonder why Time called Instagram "one of the smartest acquisitions ever."[131]

Why did Facebook acquire WhatsApp?

In 2014, Facebook made waves by acquiring the hyper-popular messaging app WhatsApp for $19 billion — that's $42 for each of WhatsApp's 450 million users at the time,[132] and vastly more than Facebook paid for Instagram. But why did Facebook spend so much on a company that many Americans hadn't even heard of,[133] especially when Facebook already had its own Messenger app?

The first reason is precisely because Americans hadn't heard of WhatsApp. WhatsApp is pretty similar to Facebook Messenger in that they both allow real-time text messaging over the internet.[134] But WhatsApp is huge in markets where Facebook and Facebook Messenger are weaker,[135] especially in developing countries like Brazil, Indonesia, and South Africa.[136] (Interestingly, the only major markets where WhatsApp hasn't taken off are China, where it's banned,[137] and the US, where mobile carriers made SMS much cheaper than data.[138])

By buying WhatsApp, Facebook made a smart defensive play. WhatsApp was strong in the exact countries where Facebook was weak, so the purchase shored up Facebook's international presence.[139] In other words, WhatsApp was no longer a competitor; people who were using one of Facebook's main rivals now belonged to Facebook anyway![140]

The second reason is data. WhatsApp could provide Facebook troves of personal data on its millions of users — especially in developing markets — which would help Facebook better target its ads and services.[141] Targeted ads, of course, are how Facebook makes money.[142]

A third reason is photos, which should sound familiar from the Instagram case. Dominating the world of photos is one of Facebook's core goals,[143] and it had reason to worry about WhatsApp. WhatsApp users sent 500 million pictures a day in 2014, which was more than Facebook and Instagram combined.[144] Snapping up WhatsApp was a smart way for Facebook to regain dominance over photos.

Pundits have put forward many more reasons,[145] but the last one we'll cover is dominance of the mobile space. Mobile is particularly critical for Facebook, since 91% of Facebook's ad revenue comes from mobile.[146] So, without a mobile operating system of its own (unlike its archrivals, Apple and Google), Facebook realized it needed to control as many popular apps as possible.[147] So it makes sense why they'd want WhatsApp, which is consistently among the most popular apps on Android and iOS.[148]

In short, buying WhatsApp filled several of Facebook's biggest holes: developing countries, data, mobile, and photos. It was an expensive but savvy move — Business Insider even praised the WhatsApp purchase as Facebook's "best ever."[149]

Chapter 10.
Emerging Markets

So far in *Swipe to Unlock*, we've focused on tech in Western world. Now, let's branch out and explore how Western tech companies are trying to expand into the rest of the world — and how tech companies from these emerging markets are bursting onto the global stage.

Which countries do Western tech companies most want to expand into?

In 2018, Facebook announced that its growth had flatlined in the US and Canada and had, in fact, begun shrinking in Europe.[1] Instead, most of Facebook's growth was coming from the developing world,[2] with India, Indonesia, and the Philippines leading the pack.[3]

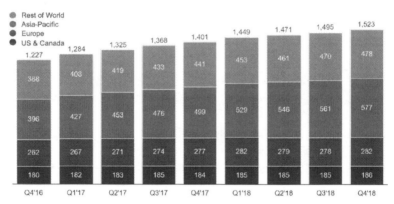

Facebook's daily active users around the world. Facebook's user growth in the US, Canada, and Europe (bottom bars) ground to a halt in 2018. Source: Facebook[4]

Facebook isn't alone — most major Western tech companies have realized they've saturated Western markets, running out of room for growth.[5] So it should be no surprise that, in addition to Facebook, giants like Google,[6] Amazon,[7] and Uber[8] are investing heavily in developing countries. But of the dozens and dozens of developing countries in the world, which ones are ripe for Western tech companies to break into?

We think each of the five key regions in the developing world— China, India, Southeast Asia (also known as SEA or ASEAN), Latin America (or LatAm), and Africa — is at a different stage in the game. We can arrange them on a spectrum from "too late" to "too early" for Western tech companies to get into:

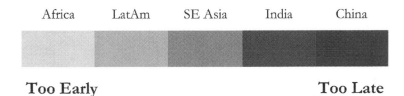

| Africa | LatAm | SE Asia | India | China |

Too Early   **Too Late**

Our model of how ripe each region of the developing world is for the entrance of Western tech companies. It's too late to get into China and too early for Africa — and it's a spectrum between them.

Let's step through each of the five regions and explore why we assigned the ratings we did.

China: walled off

Western tech companies have long wanted to expand into China, which has an explosive economy and more Internet users than any other country.[9] But Western software companies, to put it mildly, have not been successful in China. This is mostly because of the Great Firewall of China, a set of restrictions on the internet put in place by the Chinese government to restrict the flow of information in and out of the country. Most major Western websites — including Google, Facebook, YouTube, and Wikipedia — are blocked, stifling these countries' attempts to gain users in China.[10]

Western software companies have tried to strike a deal with the Chinese government to get through the Great Firewall, but to little avail. Despite years of Mark Zuckerberg's maneuvering, Facebook is still blocked in China;[11] Google twice floated plans to unveil a Chinese search engine but backed down both times;[12] Uber tried expanding into China but found it too expensive and sold its Chinese operations to local rival Didi Chuxing.[13] What's more, Chinese law requires tech companies to hand over user data to the government,[14] which has made Facebook[15] and Google[16] reluctant to try expanding again.

One big reason why Western software companies are likely to stay blocked is that, behind the protection of the Great Firewall, China's homegrown tech companies have grown massive.[17] These companies have been doing great: in 2018 China had 9 of the world's 20 biggest tech companies, second only to the US with the remaining 11.[18]

Many of these companies mirror American giants. The e-commerce giant Alibaba is like the Chinese Amazon.[19] Tencent is the world's biggest gaming company[20] and the creator of the juggernaut social media app WeChat,[21] so it's a parallel to Facebook. Baidu dominates Chinese search[22] like Google dominates the rest of the world. Keeping homegrown tech companies insulated from foreign competition has clearly worked for China, so they'll probably want to keep it that way.

Hardware is another story, though. Apple has managed to succeed in China: it sells more iPhones in China than in the US.[23] Apple's China business isn't without challenges, though: the iPhone has seen rising competition from Chinese phone manufacturer Xiaomi,[24] and political tension between the US and China has harmed iPhone sales.[25]

Interestingly, despite being blocked from China, Facebook still manages to make money in the country: a tenth of Facebook's global revenue comes from China.[26] This is because Chinese companies are eager to advertise to Facebook's international customers, buying billions of dollars in Facebook ads a year.[27]

So while some companies have managed to grow businesses in China, it is — and will likely remain — next to impossible for internet companies to get any users whatsoever there.

India: the grand prize

While Western tech companies have limited options in China, they are salivating over the world's largest democracy.

India loves smartphones: there are more smartphone users in India than there are people in the US[28] and over a billion smartphones throughout the country.[29] (India has more smartphones than toilets![30]) The reason smartphones are so popular in India is that most Indians didn't experience the internet until the smartphone boom of the 2000s was well underway, meaning that India skipped the PC era and went straight to mobile.[31]

It didn't hurt that, in 2016, the Indian telecom provider Jio announced a plan that offered dirt-cheap data, forcing its competitors to reduce the price of a gigabyte of data from an average of $4.50 to just 15¢.[32] This poured jet fuel on India's growing mobile economy, turning a country originally conservative with data into a land of avid WhatsApp'ers and YouTube viewers.[33]

Unlike China, India remains pretty open to foreign firms, and there are no homegrown titans to challenge Western tech companies. So Western tech companies have been investing billions of dollars in India in a bid to win the hearts and minds of India's smartphone-loving billions.[34]

Facebook has had "Lite" version of its core app for India ever since 2009,[35] and it bought WhatsApp in 2014 in large part because of the messaging service's popularity in India.[36] Google announced a lightweight version of its core Search product, called Google Go,[37] in 2017[38] and announced an India-focused mobile payments app called Tez (now called Google Pay[39]) that same year.[40] Amazon Prime has also grown explosively in India since 2017.[41]

Releasing apps in India isn't just a matter of repackaging Western apps; they need to be tailored to the market. Localization is especially key[42] — India has 29 languages with more than a million native speakers[43] — so just releasing an app in English (or even Hindi) isn't enough. Other modifications Western apps have needed include preferring tapping to typing (since typing on phones is cumbersome), reducing data usage,[44] and even reading articles aloud (to handle lower literacy rates in India).[45]

Google Go, Google's India-focused app. It also includes links to web apps, probably because Indians are more used to apps (like WhatsApp) than the idea of searching the web. Source: Mashable[46]

Western giants' incredible investment in India seems to be paying off. Facebook's flagship app has millions more users in India than in the US,[47] and Google's Android controls over 70% of the gigantic Indian mobile phone market.[48]

Southeast Asia: the fight is on

While the contours of the battles for China and India are pretty well-defined, Southeast Asia — including Indonesia, Thailand, and the Philippines — is anyone's game. This area has a lot in common with India:[49] it's the world's 3rd-largest market in terms of internet users, and people here spend twice as much time on their phones (nearly 4 hours a day) as Americans (just 2 hours a day).[50]

Southeast Asia is right in China's backyard, so many of the Chinese titans have started backing local startups here. But it's still open enough that Western companies can break in, so Southeast Asia has become to number-one battleground between the Western and Eastern giants.[51]

Western tech companies have tested a few apps tailored to Southeast Asia — like a social commerce and payment platform from Facebook[52] — but nowhere near as many as in India. Indeed, several India-focused apps, like Google's Tez (now Google Pay) payments platform[53] and Android Go,[54] have now been launched in Southeast Asia. (The general pattern is that India is Western companies' blueprint for how to tackle the developing world, and after products get traction there the next stop is usually Southeast Asia.[55])

The most unique opportunity for Western tech companies in Southeast Asia is in e-commerce. There aren't many brick-and-mortar retail stores here — Southeast Asia has 46 times less retail space per person than the US![56] Local e-commerce startups, such as Singapore-based Lazada[57] and Indonesia-based Tokopedia,[58] have done well, so Western companies will probably want to emulate them.

With its young population, growing economy, relatively stable governance, and ideal level of development (not under- or over-developed), Southeast Asia is shaping up to be a "Game of Thrones"-like battle between international tech giants.[59] And because the region is made of a patchwork of countries with very different laws, Southeast Asia will be less winner-take-all than more unified markets like India (which has a consistent set of laws across the country), meaning this region will remain a toss-up for a long time to come.

Latin America: up and coming

While the best time to get into India was yesterday, and the best time to get into Southeast Asia is today, the best time to get into Latin America is definitely tomorrow.

Western tech companies haven't made many huge splashes here, but it's been on their radar for a while: Google's social network Orkut, for instance, was the dominant social media platform in Brazil from 2008[60] to 2012.[61]

The potential is tremendous, though. The region's GDP is almost as big as China's,[62] and Latin American countries are big internet users: Brazil ranks 4th on the list of countries with the most internet users, and Mexico ranks 9th.[63]

As the Orkut story might hint, social media is huge here: Brazil has been called the "social media capital of the universe"[64] because 97% of all internet-connected Brazilians use social media.[65] And as mobile phones and 4G see massive uptake among younger Latin Americans,[66] mobile social media is likely to become a major trend here. Android[67] and WhatsApp[68] are already dominant here.

The big red flag is that Latin America's internet infrastructure isn't up to scratch, which could slow future growth.[69]

Africa: not ripe yet

Finally, we'll turn to Africa, which is seen as not yet developed enough for serious entry by the Western tech giants. Africa's internet infrastructure is also considered below-par[70] — the internet here is four times slower than in developed markets.[71] It should be no surprise, then, that internet penetration in Africa is almost half of the worldwide average.[72] Phones and data plans are also too expensive for the average African.[73]

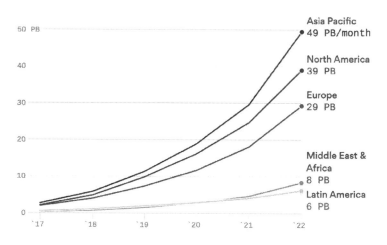

Forecasted internet traffic

IPv6 traffic by region in Petabytes per month, 2017–22

Asia Pacific
49 PB/month

North America
39 PB

Europe
29 PB

Middle East & Africa
8 PB

Latin America
6 PB

50 PB
40
30
20
10
0

'17 '18 '19 '20 '21 '22

Internet infrastructure in Latin America and Africa is weak, raising red flags about future growth. Source: Axios[74]

While smartphones may not have taken off in Africa, feature phones are huge.[75] M-Pesa, which lets people send money with feature phones, has over 18 million users in Kenya, a country of just 50 million.[76] The feature phone operating system KaiOS, which also powers some feature phones made by India's Jio, thinks Africa still has tremendous growth potential for feature phones.[77]

The lack of internet infrastructure has made things hard for Western software companies. Their response has been to invest in internet connectivity. Facebook is famous for its internet.org project, also known as Free Basics. This program has partnered with telecom companies in sub-Saharan Africa to offer free internet access to Africans. The catch, though, is that only certain websites (notably including Facebook apps!) can be accessed for free.

Supporters think this is a great way to get Africans online, while detractors think it's a cynical move to give Facebook an unfair leg up.[78] (Free Basics has been rolled out throughout the developing world, and it's seen mixed reviews: India banned Free Basics for violating net neutrality, for instance.[79])

How do Kenyans pay for everything with feature phones?

We just mentioned that Africa's tech scene isn't very well-developed. But in Kenya, you can pay school fees, take out loans, and even pay your rent with a feature phone. Mobile payments are so popular in Kenya that the country has been named "the world's unlikely leader in mobile payments."[80] But how and why did that happen?

The problem with banking in developing countries

The main reason mobile banking has taken off in developing countries is that many people don't have bank accounts. In the developing world, financial literacy is a problem, many people don't have the necessary IDs to start a bank account, banking infrastructure is poor, women aren't empowered to handle their finances,[81] and people flat-out don't trust banks with their money.[82]

So it should come as no surprise that two billion people around the world, mostly in developing countries, don't have bank accounts.[83]

In the West, people have been using credit cards, debit cards, and ATMs for decades.[84] But to use these tools, you have to have a bank account, trust the bank, and know how to operate the banking system. Without those prerequisites, the Western finance system doesn't work well.

That's why cash has traditionally been the dominant form of payment in developing countries.[85] But of course cash comes with its downsides too: it's easy to steal, it's hard to carry around, transactions are slow if you don't have exact change, and you can't take back a payment if something fraudulent happened.

But then phones and a radically new way to pay came around.

M-Pesa

In 2007, just as feature phones were taking off in Africa, the Kenyan telecom company Safaricom launched a money-transfer service called M-Pesa, which lets people send money with a text.[86] The app was launched in Kenya and has become incredibly popular in that country: two-thirds of Kenyan adults use M-Pesa, and a quarter of Kenya's gross national product flows through it.[87]

You can think of M-Pesa as Venmo minus the smartphones, internet, and bank account. With Venmo, you load money into your account from your bank, send money to friends with an app, and "cash out" by sending money back to your bank. Meanwhile, with M-Pesa, you load cash into your account at an M-Pesa outlet (there are 65,000 of them in Kenya, usually in gas stations or corner stores), send money to friends with a text, and withdraw cash by going to another outlet.[88]

In other words, M-Pesa requires nothing but your phone[89] (and not even a smartphone — a feature phone will do just fine) and some cash. M-Pesa has even been around longer than Venmo, which only launched in 2009![90]

An M-Pesa outlet in Kenya, where you can deposit and withdraw cash into your M-Pesa account. Source: WorldRemit Comms via Flickr[91]

M-Pesa was an instant hit with Kenyans who worked in cities and wanted to send money home to rural villages. Rural Kenyans largely didn't have bank accounts, so checks or wire transfers wouldn't work. Plus, traveling to the backcountry was expensive, sending anything in the mail was prone to failure because postal infrastructure was bad, and sending cash was risky in any case.

But, even in 2007, over half of Kenyans had access to a mobile phone — and so, with M-Pesa, workers finally had a way to send money to rural family.[92] M-Pesa has been so good, in fact, that, according to one study, rural households' income grew 5 to 30% once they started using M-Pesa.[93]

M-Pesa has since expanded into loans, savings, and merchant payments — all without bank accounts. In 2018 Safaricom announced a partnership with Western Union that would let

M-Pesa users send money to Western Union users and vice versa, meaning that a Kenyan could use M-Pesa to send money to a German whose bank uses Western Union.[94]

With 30 million users across 3 continents, M-Pesa's future looks bright — it's a sign of how much mobile payments can grow with even the simplest technologies.[95]

How did WeChat become China's "official" app?

In the US, you might use Google Maps to find a restaurant, Uber to get a ride there, Apple Pay to pay for your meal, Yelp to review the restaurant, and Facebook Messenger to tell your friends about it. In China, you'd use Tencent's WeChat app for all those things.[96]

In fact, you can do everything from booking doctor's appointments to calling cabs to paying bills on WeChat, which started life as a messaging app but has had mountains of features added on top of it.[97] It's such an essential tool that 900 million people use the app[98] — in fact, many consider it the "official" app of China.[99]

It's hard to find any other app that dominates its country more than WeChat. How did WeChat do it?

Why WeChat grew

We can think of three big reasons why WeChat has become the "Swiss army-knife" app of China.[100]

First, WeChat knew how to create fun, viral features. Shortly after its founding in 2010, WeChat started letting you shake your phone to randomly connect with other users. You could also write a digital "message in a bottle" and send it to a random WeChat user in the hopes they'd respond.[101] These features might be odd by Western standards, but Chinese users loved them and started adopting WeChat in droves.[102]

Most famously, in 2014 the app digitized the ancient tradition of *hongbao*, where Chinese people send red envelopes full of money to each other for special occasions like Lunar New Year.[103] People loved sending the envelopes to friends, and since people already had friends on WeChat (it was a messaging app, after all), everyone started using the feature. Plus, it provided a big incentive for new people to join WeChat ("get an account on this app so I can send you money" never fails).[104]

What's more, WeChat made it a game — you can send random amounts of money to friends, which makes users eager to open any *hongbao* sent their way on WeChat.[105] There's even a game where you can send money to a group chat — but only the first member of the group to open the chat gets the money.[106] That game itself made people check their WeChats obsessively, never wanting to miss a *hongbao* sent to their groups.[107]

The brilliant part was that anyone who wanted to send *hongbaos* had to connect their bank accounts to WeChat. Once people had done that, it was easy for WeChat to get people to start using WeChat's payment system, aptly named WeChat Pay, to buy movie tickets, pay bills, hail taxis, and such.[108] As soon as the *hongbao* feature launched, the number of WeChat Pay users mushroomed from 30 million to 100 million.[109] The feature has even been credited with helping WeChat Pay overtake Alipay, its archrival payment system that's actually been around longer.[110] And the growth of WeChat Pay made WeChat more than just a messaging app — it set WeChat on the path toward becoming *the* app for everything in China.

The second reason for WeChat's success was simple: it was in the right place at the right time. In 2010, just before WeChat launched publicly, just 36 million smartphones were sold in China, but just two years later that number had exploded to 214 million.[111] And, since WeChat quickly got a foothold on smartphones in 2010, it could grow as fast as smartphones did.

The third big reason WeChat grew was that it forged a strong relationship with the Chinese government, which helped fend off foreign rivals. The Chinese government demands that Tencent hand over user data and not use encryption[112] — which Western companies might not like doing for fear of backlash in other countries.[113] But because WeChat does what the government says, the government has helped WeChat out by banning competing apps like Facebook Messenger, WhatsApp, and the Korean messaging app Line in China.[114]

This cooperation is so deep that the Chinese government announced in 2018 that it would integrate WeChat with China's electronic ID system[115] — which helps the government grow the ID program and makes WeChat even more of a must-have app. Partnering with the government has paid dividends.

Lessons for the West

While WeChat hasn't seen much usage outside China — perhaps because it's so tailored to the culture and laws of China — it's influenced a lot of Western technology.

Most notably, WeChat kicked off the concept of a messaging app as an operating system. In the West, Android or iOS is your operating system, and if you want to get a hospital appointment or invest money, you have to install apps from Apple's App Store or Google's Play Store.

But in China, WeChat is really your operating system — anything you want to do, including getting that hospital appointment and investing money,[116] can be done through WeChat "accounts"[117] or "mini-programs."[118] There's little need to install other apps when one app does it all. The benefit is that, with WeChat, your identity and payment information can be reused across every account and mini-program,[119] whereas in the West you have to have a separate account for Uber, Venmo, PayPal, Amazon, and almost every other app (and you have to re-enter your credit card in each app, to boot!)

So it doesn't really matter whether you have an iPhone or an Android, as long as it runs WeChat.[120] This is problematic for Apple, since its high-quality apps and iOS — which usually keep people hooked on iPhones — no longer matter. Instead, Chinese phone makers like Xiaomi can launch Android phones that offer similar hardware to iPhones at a lower price.[121] At that point, iPhones' only unique feature in China is that they're luxury status symbols.[122]

WeChat has also inspired Facebook, which has always wanted to control an operating system but instead has had to play by whatever rules Google and Apple set for Android and iOS.[123] So Facebook has wanted to make Messenger the WeChat of the West — because if people does everything through Messenger, Facebook can control the entire experience and not care about Android or iOS. That's probably why Facebook has crammed so many features into Messenger in recent years, from payments[124] to games[125] to chatbots for businesses.[126]

As you can tell, WeChat impacts the entire globe — and people around the world can learn from it.

How can you pay for almost anything with a QR code in Asia?

In China, paying street performers with cash has become practically unheard of. You pay for everything by scanning a QR code (those squares full of jumbled-up black-and-white tiles) with your phone.[127] You can also pay panhandlers and make wedding gifts by scanning QR codes.[128] And in Singaporean food courts, you'll often see more people their phones up to QR codes than people paying at cash registers.[129]

So how and why can you pay with your phone in so many places in Asia? And why with a QR code, of all things?

QR codes are everywhere in East and Southeast Asia — even street vendors now let you pay for things with Alipay or WeChat by scanning their QR codes. Source: WalktheChat via Twitter[130]

WeChat Pay & Alipay

In many parts of China, you don't have to carry a wallet around anymore — your phone is enough to pay for restaurants, bike sharing, cell phone service, and even rent.[131] This is because of the massive mobile payment services we touched on earlier: Tencent's WeChat Pay, which has over 900 million users, and Alibaba's Alipay, with over 500 million.[132]

Unlike M-Pesa, WeChat Pay and Alipay require bank accounts, phone numbers, and official IDs,[133] and you have to have a smartphone to make payments. But unlike Africa, almost everyone in China has a smartphone.[134]

Everyone from street vendors to fancy restaurants in China accepts payments via QR code: scan a code with WeChat or Alipay and you can send someone money instantly.[135] The reason QR codes have taken off is how easy it is to get started. Anyone can print out a QR code — you don't need credit card readers, cash registers, or any other special hardware to become a merchant.

WeChat Pay and Alipay have mostly been confined to China so far, but in 2018 WeChat Pay expanded into Malaysia — so these apps are likely to keep expanding.[136]

Grab & Go-Jek

QR code payment is getting popular in Southeast Asia too. To understand why, you have to first understand how mobile payments there have taken off.

The two biggest Southeast Asian mobile payment systems are the Singaporean startup Grab and the Indonesian startup Go-Jek.[137] (Incidentally, Grab is backed by Alibaba[138] while Go-Jek is backed by Tencent[139] — so while they may dominate Southeast Asia they aren't competing with the Chinese payment giants.)

Grab and Go-Jek are ridesharing companies: Go-Jek lets you hail motorcycles[140] and dominates Indonesia,[141] while Grab lets you call taxis just like Uber does (its founders explicitly wanted to make "Uber for Asia")[142] and dominates the rest of Southeast Asia. Besides that, they're pretty similar apps.[143]

Ridesharing is great, but the reason these startups have gotten so much hype is that their millions of users have now entered their payment information into the apps and started storing money in the apps' digital wallets.[144] Getting people to store money in your app is a big hurdle — but once you've gotten them to do that, whether with a clever *hongbao* promotion or making them pay for ridesharing, you can start selling them anything.

And that's exactly what Grab and Go-Jek have been doing.[145] You can now buy food, send packages, get pills delivered to your door, get your air conditioner fixed, get your laundry done, and even get a massage on Go-Jek.[146] (What do all these features have in common? They're all selling you stuff, which is why having the mobile payments already set up is key. You might not go through the hassle of setting up payments in an app just to get a massage, but if you already have money in the app, it becomes way more tempting to get that massage.)

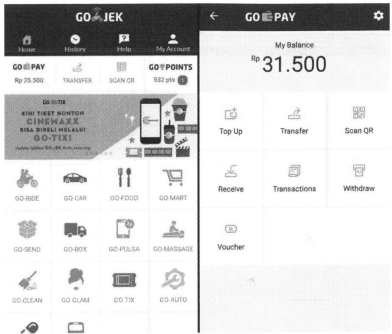

The Indonesian app Go-Jek, originally just for hailing motorcycles, has expanded to let you pay friends (GO-PAY), get your makeup done (GO-GLAM), and get your house cleaned (GO-CLEAN). Source: Tech in Asia[147]

And, of course, you can scan a QR code to pay for something.

Grab and Go-Jek have become tremendously successful. For instance, Uber tried expanding into Southeast Asia but got outmaneuvered and had to sell its operations to Grab.[148] (Not bad for a company that wanted to become the "Uber of Asia"!)

But the battle for Southeast Asia is still red-hot. Go-Jek and Grab have expanded into each other's home turf, with Go-Jek moving into Singapore[149] and Grab growing into Indonesia.[150] Besides each other, they're also battling smaller local payment systems like PayNow and Dash in Singapore, Malaysia's Razer Pay,[151] the Philippines' InstaPay, and VNPay in Vietnam.[152]

Paytm

QR codes and mobile payments in India aren't as far along as in China or Southeast Asia, but they're getting there, led by the mobile payment startup Paytm.

Paytm began life as a mobile payment system, which let you load in money from a bank account (like WeChat Pay) or with cash (like M-Pesa) and then pay it out to friends and businesses. Paytm got a big boost when the Indian government in 2016 "demonetized" 500- and 1000-rupee notes (then worth about $7 and $14 respectively), making them no longer legal tender and forcing people to get new notes.[153] This gave Indians an extra reason to experiment with cashless payment systems — and so Paytm took off, growing to over 150 million users overnight.[154]

But, like Grab and Go-Jek, Paytm has since decided to try to become the next WeChat, offering ever more features and selling ever more things. You can now send messages, pay bills, shop online, and play games on Paytm. It even has started allowing "mini-programs."[155] And, of course, you can now pay just by scanning a QR code.[156]

In short, mobile payments have taken off all around Asia because they're the center of a clever business model: once you get people's payment info, you can try to become the next WeChat and utterly dominate your country's tech scene.

How do Western and Eastern tech companies' strategies differ?

It's been said that American and Chinese tech companies are locked in a war over the developing world,[157] and China and the US are widely considered to be in a "race" to dominate artificial intelligence,[158] telecommunications tech,[159] and even the future of the internet.[160]

But it's not like the two sides are copies of each other. As you've seen this chapter, Western and Eastern tech companies are very different beasts — but how exactly are they different, and what impact does that have on the countries' rivalry?

Direct and indirect

If you live in India or Southeast Asia, chances are good that you've heard of Google, Facebook, Amazon, and other Western tech titans because you've seen or used their apps. Meanwhile, you've probably never heard of Chinese mega-corporations like Alibaba and Tencent — even though these companies are, behind the scenes, backing dozens of the most popular apps in your country.

This speaks to a larger trend. When Western companies expand into emerging markets, they tend to just import their existing apps and business models.[161] People around the developing world use the same Facebook, iPhone, and YouTube that Europeans and North Americans do. Even when Western companies release products tailored to the developing world, they're just spin-offs of the main apps. Consider Google Go and Android Go, Google's tweaked versions of Google Search and Android aimed at India[162] — they may look and feel a bit different from the originals, but at their core they're just tweaks to the existing formula.

Meanwhile, Chinese companies usually don't just drop tweaked versions of Chinese apps into other markets. Instead, they tend to invest in local businesses that create apps and business models custom-made for local markets. For instance, Alibaba hasn't set up its namesake Alibaba e-commerce website outside China.[163]

But Alibaba has bought stakes in a variety of companies that handle e-commerce-related things like online shopping, mobile payments, and delivery:[164] India's Paytm,[165] Singapore's Grab,[166] Indonesia's e-commerce startup Tokopedia,[167] and Pakistan's e-commerce startup Daraz.[168] Usually, Alibaba invests enough money in these startups to have some say over the company's future, but it doesn't splash the Alibaba branding all over them.

Tencent does something similar. It has tried to expand WeChat into other countries, but it typically has done so through close partnerships with a local companies. To try expanding into Malaysia and Thailand, Tencent partnered with the local ride-hailing app Easy Taxi to launch a taxi-hailing feature in WeChat (but only for Malaysia and Thailand).[169] To grow into Singapore, it partnered with Singaporean e-commerce startup Lazada to add special Lazada features into WeChat in Singapore.[170]

Like Alibaba, Tencent has also invested in a wide range of startups in the developing world, like Indonesia's Go-Jek,[171] the Indian ride-hailing app Ola,[172] and the Indian fantasy sports platform Dream11.[173] It's been especially aggressive in the gaming space, investing in gaming companies from South Korea to Iceland to Japan[174] — including Tencent's famous investment in the makers of Fortnite.[175] (These investments could also be future lures to get people on WeChat.)

The difference between Western and Eastern strategies was at its clearest in India, where Amazon and Alibaba both tried to conquer the e-commerce market in the mid-2010s. While Amazon tried to build up Prime itself in India starting in 2014, Alibaba's move was to invest in the local startup Paytm in 2015.[176]

Why the difference?

The difference in approaches stems from a difference in business models. Western companies have long focused on creating business models that can be grown, or scaled, easily. Whether you're selling ads (like Google and Facebook) or selling phones (like Apple), the same approach works anywhere in the world: every company in the world wants to sell ads, and most people in the world want to buy phones. So Western apps and business models can work the same way anywhere in the world, with few changes required except maybe the language.[177]

Meanwhile, Chinese firms have set themselves apart with great payments and delivery in countries where physical infrastructure hasn't always been great. The problem here is that payments and delivery work very differently in different countries — as the Economist puts it, becoming a distribution expert in the city-state of Singapore doesn't teach you anything about delivering items to Indonesia's thousands of islands. Since the ideal solutions are tailored to each country, Chinese companies tend to let entrepreneurs in those countries build tailored companies and buy them once they're ready.[178]

Both strategies clearly work. American firms' incredible scalability gives them a huge head start whenever they enter a new market: when Amazon moved into India, for instance, it already had a gigantic logistics infrastructure, payments system, brand name, and relationships with other companies in place.[179] Meanwhile, by tailoring products and business models to each country (which is obviously hard to scale), Chinese companies can be sure they'll be well-positioned wherever they go.

However, both strategies have their downsides. While American tech companies' products and business models might be pretty good in most countries, they might not be perfect for any given country. (Consider how Google released Google Go and Android Go in India — it was a sign that the standard Google app and Android weren't perfect fits for India.[180]) And Chinese companies end up backing a patchwork of startups that often compete against each other: Alibaba backs the Southeast Asian e-commerce startups Tokopedia[181] and Lazada,[182] which compete in many of the same countries across the region.[183]

Meeting of the minds

So neither strategy is necessarily better or worse than the other. In fact, Western and Eastern companies have started borrowing strategies from each other's playbooks. Walmart bought India's e-commerce giant Flipkart in 2018[184] instead of, say, just trying to set up a bunch of Walmarts and online delivery itself in India. Google, in a typically-Eastern move, started investing in the Indonesian ride-hailing company Go-Jek[185] and Indian e-commerce startup Fynd in 2018.[186] That same year, Alibaba announced several globally-available cloud computing products, marking Alibaba's first Alibaba-branded product launch outside China.[187]

So while it's not clear who will win the so-called "tech war"[188] between the East and West, there's a sign that companies on both sides are picking up tips from their competitors abroad.

Chapter 11.
Technology Policy

The internet has become the primary way we shop, read the news, communicate, research, and do business. It should be no surprise, then, that the world of technology has come crashing headfirst into long-standing policy and legal debates around antitrust, free speech, privacy, and more.

In this chapter, we'll look into a few cases when these debates have boiled over into policy battles and explore how governments have begun regulating tech companies. Buckle up.

How can Comcast sell your browsing history?

In 2016, the Federal Communications Commission (FCC), the US government's department that regulates telecommunications and the internet, released rules that forced internet service providers (ISPs) to get your consent before selling your browsing history to advertisers.[1] But in 2017, Congress passed a bill that killed these "broadband privacy" regulations.[2] In other words, the 2017 ruling lets ISPs sell your information whenever and however they like.[3] Consumer advocates were outraged.[4]

But who exactly are these ISPs? What data do they have about you? And what's wrong with them selling that data? Let's break it down.

Nonstop surveillance

Whenever you connect to the internet over Wi-Fi or watch TV over cable, you're consuming so-called "broadband" content.[5] Companies called internet service providers, or ISPs, deliver that content to you; in other words, they're the people who provide your cable and home internet.[6] The largest ISPs in the US include Comcast, AT&T, Verizon, CenturyLink, Cox,[7] and Spectrum.[8]

Don't confuse these with the telephone companies that bring you 4G and mobile service. Those include Verizon, AT&T, Sprint, and T-Mobile.[9] (Note that Verizon and AT&T are on both lists!)

Because ISPs sit between you and every website you visit, they can track your entire browsing history. Then they can sell this information, along with demographic information like your age and location, to advertisers, who can use the data to target ads at you.[10] This is a treasure trove of information that dwarfs even what Facebook and Google have on you.[11] Privacy advocates say that ISPs can even hijack your Google searches or inject ads into websites you browse.[12] One particularly infamous example was Verizon's "supercookie," a tracker that Verizon once installed on all its phones that tracked every website you visited without offering a way to opt out.[13] (Verizon killed the supercookie, but privacy advocates say it could return.[14])

A game of Monopoly

If you don't like what the ISPs are doing, tough luck. Thanks to a spate of mergers and acquisitions, ISPs have monopolies in much of the country[15]: the Federal Communications Commission (FCC) estimated that 75% of American households have zero or one option for high-speed ISPs — in other words, their ISP has a monopoly.[16] And, predictably, the monopolies have led to slower internet connections and higher prices.[17] For instance, AT&T has a monopoly in Cupertino, California but competes with another ISP in Austin, Texas — and AT&T charges consumers in Cupertino $40 more for the exact same basic service![18]

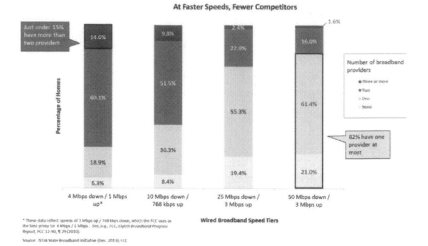

At Faster Speeds, Fewer Competitors

More than three-quarters of Americans have zero or one choice of ISPs for high-speed internet, defined as 25 Mbps or more. That's a troubling sign of a monopolistic market. Source: FCC[19]

Unfortunately, these monopolies seem tough to break up or regulate due to lax antitrust regulations and the high barriers to entry in the telecom business.[20] Setting up the massive infrastructure required to deliver the internet is so hard that even Google had trouble doing it. Google tried creating its own super-fast ISP called Google Fiber, but it encountered difficulty and significantly scaled down in 2017.[21]

Because ISPs are nearly monopolistic, their information-selling habits are particularly dangerous for consumers. If your ISPs are selling your browsing history but you don't like it, you're out of luck — there aren't many other options besides ditching the internet entirely.[22]

Regulation — or not

Before 2016, there were few regulations against ISPs selling user data to marketers.[23] But in 2016, the Federal Communications Commission (FCC) passed a rule saying that ISPs had to get explicit opt-in permission from customers before they could sell people's browsing history to marketers.[24] Broadband privacy advocates celebrated the victory.[25]

But in 2017, a new FCC chairman named Ajit Pai came to power, and with his support Congress axed the rule.[26] That meant that ISPs could continue selling people's data to marketers without their consent.[27]

Consumer advocates decried this ruling, calling it a power grab by ISPs and an invasion of consumer privacy.[28] Supporters of the move said it was only fair, since the data-selling regulations didn't apply to Facebook or Google, which also make billions by using data to target ads.[29] They said that ISPs needed ad-targeting power to compete with Google and Facebook.

There's no end in sight to this battle. But fortunately, there's at least one funny result. After the FCC rolled back the broadband privacy rules, the tech news site ZDNet filed a Freedom of Information Act request asking to see the browsing history of the new FCC chairman Ajit Pai, who fought for the new rules. The FCC said it didn't have any information.[30]

How does free mobile data hurt consumers?

If you live in the UK and use Virgin Media as your mobile carrier, good news: you can use WhatsApp, Facebook Messenger, and Twitter without paying for the data they use.

Virgin Media offers "data-free" use of WhatsApp, Facebook Messenger, and Twitter, but is it really good for consumers? Source: Virgin Media[31]

Similarly, in the US, if you have AT&T you can use AT&T's streaming service, DirecTV Now, for free — no data charges will apply, no matter how many videos you watch.[32]

This practice, where using certain apps doesn't count toward your data bill, is called "zero rating."[33] It sounds great — who doesn't like unlimited texting and binge watching? But one major study found that zero rating actually made wireless data *more* expensive for consumers as a whole.[34] But how?

It turns out that zero rating is one of the most prominent fronts in the ongoing policy debate over net neutrality.[35] Let's dive into net neutrality before explaining what happened with zero rating.

Net neutrality

Net neutrality, simply put, is the principle that ISPs should treat all data equally. No bit of data should be given preferential treatment; no movie or Tweet or GIF should be allowed to move faster than others or, in zero rating's case, be given to consumers more cheaply than others (which would make that data more attractive to consumers than other data).[36]

Fundamentally, ISPs control access to the internet; everything you consume on the internet flows through the likes of Verizon and Comcast. This gives ISPs a lot of power — they can put their thumb on the scale to privilege certain apps or websites by, say, slowing down their competitors' data. But if ISPs get to tilt the playing field in favor of whatever companies pay them the most, that's a huge loss for consumers. The internet loses its openness, innovation and competition is restricted, and economic growth gets slowed.[37]

Concretely, net neutrality calls to end three practices that ISPs do to unfairly exploit their power for profit.

First is "blocking," when ISPs outright ban traffic on their networks. The most infamous example is when AT&T tried to ban FaceTime for customers who didn't pay for a more expensive data plan.[38] This was a transparent way to force customers to pay AT&T more. Customers locked into contracts with AT&T would have no option but to upgrade if they wanted to use FaceTime, since all their FaceTime data would flow through AT&T.

Blocking a website entirely is pretty obvious, so many ISPs prefer a more subtle approach: "throttling." Throttling is when

ISPs slow down content from particular websites, often competitors'.[39] In 2013 and 2014, Comcast and Verizon slowed down content from Netflix,[40] perhaps because they wanted to give a boost to their own video-streaming services.[41] The throttling got so bad that Netflix had to pay Comcast and Verizon to stop.[42] Thus, Comcast and Verizon used their power over customers to give their own products an unfair advantage and squeeze money from Netflix.

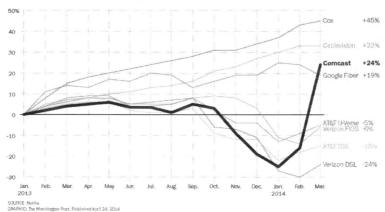

% change in Netflix download speed since Jan. 2013, by I.S.P.

In a case of throttling, Netflix saw sudden speed drops on Comcast until it paid up in January 2014, at which point its speed skyrocketed. Source: Technical.ly[43]

Third is "paid prioritization," which is when an ISP strikes a deal with a website to send that website's information faster than its competitors'.[44] Paid prioritization, also known as a paid "fast lane," has become more common than blocking and throttling in recent years. Zero rating is a perfect example of paid prioritization — so let's dig into why it harms consumers.

Zero rating

Recall that, with zero rating, an ISP gives consumers fee-free access to certain apps, often in exchange for hefty fees from the creators of those apps.[45] That gives those apps a big edge over competitors — would you rather binge watch on a service that ran up your data bills or one that didn't?

The fundamental problem is that zero rating harms startups. Take the example of Virgin Media offering free access to WhatsApp, Facebook Messenger, and Twitter. The giant companies behind those apps could definitely afford to pay Virgin Media for that privilege. But a startup building the next great messaging app definitely could not, and so it'd be at a stark disadvantage compared to its richer competitors. The small video website Vimeo, which has just 200 employees, said it couldn't afford to keep up its zero rating deal with Deutsche Telekom, which owns T-Mobile.[46] Zero rating, in other words, favors entrenched tech giants and inhibits innovation.[47]

This gets even worse when the ISPs can promote their own products, effectively getting a free boost over competitors. AT&T's zero-rating of its own DirecTV Now video streaming service is a prime example. That program gives DirecTV Now a huge edge, locking in users and shutting out competitors. It's a good deal for customers now, but if DirecTV Now drove its competitors out of business, AT&T could just stop zero rating and hike the price for consumers, who would have nowhere else to go.[48]

As we mentioned earlier, the European nonprofit called Epicenter.works ran a study on zero rating within 30 European countries and found that, when a country allowed zero rating, wireless carriers increased prices. Countries that banned zero rating saw steady drops in the prices of wireless plans, but countries that allowed the practice actually saw an increase.[49]

Why? Once carriers can attract customers based on zero rating agreements, they no longer need to compete on price or network quality, so they no longer need to improve in those areas.[50]

The history of net neutrality

So far, we've only talked about a world where there is no net neutrality. In the US, at least, net neutrality has had a checkered past: it's been required for a few years this century, but not nearly all.

The Federal Communications Commission (FCC), which is tasked with regulating internet services, didn't regulate ISPs until 2002, when it placed them under a lax provision called Title I,[51] which didn't ban blocking, throttling, or paid prioritization.[52] Title I doesn't count as net neutrality, though.

In 2015, the FCC started regulating ISP under the stricter Title II, which bans blocking, throttling, and paid prioritization[53] — in other words, Title II enforced net neutrality. Net neutrality supporters were thrilled.[54] But then, in 2017, the new FCC chairman Ajit Pai reclassified ISPs under Title I, effectively destroying net neutrality.[55] Pai argued that forcing net neutrality made ISPs slow the expansion of speedy broadband connections[56] and that Title II was outdated.[57]

Pai might not have been the most unbiased decision maker, though: he was formerly a lawyer for Verizon![58]

How did a British doctor make Google take down search results about his malpractice?

In 2014, a British doctor asked Google to take down 50 links to newspaper articles about some botched medical procedures he had done in the past. Due to a new European law,[59] Google agreed, removing links to 3 search results that would appear if someone Googled the doctor's name.[60]

Understandably, the public was outraged. People often choose doctors based on what they find from Google searches — and if malpractice results don't show up, patients could make uninformed decisions that could harm their health.[61] Why was Google forced to comply with this request, and is this trend a force for good or bad?

The right to be forgotten

The story of forcing Google to remove unflattering links starts in Spain in 1998. That year, a man named Mario Costeja Gonzalez racked up some debts that local newspapers reported on. In 2010, he was dismayed that Google searches for his name still showed these articles that hurt his reputation, even though it was over a decade later. So he asked Google to take down the search results. This escalated into a lawsuit that reached the European Court of Justice in 2014, when the court ruled that, in the European Union, the right to privacy includes a "right to be forgotten."[62]

Under this law, if you search for your name on Google in an EU country and see a link to a website that contains "inadequate, irrelevant or no longer relevant" information about you, you can ask Google to remove that website from search results for your name.[63]

Users can ask for a takedown using a form on Google's website.[64] Google has to then decide whether or not to keep the page. The company has to weigh how much hiding the information would help the person against how important it is for the public to know the information.[65] If Google doesn't comply or the EU doesn't like their decision, the EU can take legal action against Google.[66]

If Google decides to censor search results for a particular term, it'll show you a notification at the top of the page:

> Some results may have been removed under data protection law in Europe.[67]

The "right to be forgotten" law has been invoked millions of times. Google started accepting takedown requests in May 2014, and within a month it got 50,000 takedown requests.[68] Within 3 years, Google was asked to remove over 2 million URLs, 43% of which it took down.[69] The websites most targeted for removal from search results included Facebook, YouTube, Twitter, Google Groups, Google Plus, and Instagram.[70]

Most of the takedown requests are pretty innocuous: an estimated 99% of the takedown requests were just to protect innocent people's private information.[71] For instance, a sexual assault survivor got Google to hide newspaper articles about the crime.[72] But some requests were more sinister, like the malpracticing British doctor we mentioned earlier, a politician who wanted to hide unflattering articles about his past, and a convicted criminal who wanted to remove mention of his wrongdoings.[73]

It's important to note that invoking the right to be forgotten doesn't let you flat-out delete something from the internet. Even if Google hides the link to an article from search results for your name, the link will still show up in other searches.[74] For instance, consider the British doctor: the malpractice articles wouldn't show up on a search for his name, but they might show up for a search like "British doctor malpractice." And, of course, the article would still exist on the original site. More notably, the ruling only applies to Google's European search engines. A removed search result could be gone from Google.de or Google.fr, but anyone searching on Google.com — even someone in Europe — could still see the result.[75] France's data protection authority noticed this loophole, though, and has ordered Google to remove results from all of its search engines worldwide.[76]

Forgive and forget?

Commentators around the world were outraged at the "right to be forgotten" law, saying it restricted the freedom of speech and the press.[77] Google called it a "disappointing ruling for search engines and online publishers in general,"[78] and Google cofounder Larry Page warned that the ruling could stifle internet startups.[79] Others feared that tyrannical governments could use this law as a precedent to justify mass censorship.[80] More philosophically, some observers thought it was strange that a private search engine company now has to be the judge of free speech.[81]

But supporters of the law called the right to be forgotten an individual right.[82] Some privacy advocates see it as a victory.[83] The law could also stop youthful indiscretions from coming back to haunt people forever — in this world where everything is permanently recorded on the internet, the ability to forgive and forget can be a welcome change.[84]

The debate might just boil down to a question of values, though.[85] Whereas Americans tend to value free speech above almost anything else, Europeans generally place more emphasis on the right to privacy.[86] That might explain the differing opinions on the right to be forgotten — and it hints that the battles over the law will not be forgotten anytime soon.

How did the American government create the multi-billion dollar weather industry out of thin air?

Before 1983, the only source of weather data and predictions — from temperatures to tornadoes — was from the National Weather Service, an American government agency that had been dutifully collecting data since 1870.[87] In 1983, the NWS took the unprecedented step of offering its data to third parties. Private companies could buy NWS data and use it in their own products or forecasts.[88]

Whether or not the NWS expected it, this simple move spurred the creation of a private-sector weather prediction industry.[89] The weather industry, which includes big companies like AccuWeather, the Weather Channel, and Weather Underground, is now valued at about $5 billion.[90] In other words, the US government created a $5 billion industry out of thin air just by releasing data to the public.

This is a natural partnership. Private industries can't build the satellites and radar needed to take millions of accurate weather measurements, but the government can provide this data. In exchange, weather companies create forecasts and tools that help citizens and businesses.[91] For instance, AccuWeather built software that lets them pinpoint severe weather risks so precisely that they can tell which segments of a railroad will be hit. Once, AccuWeather noticed that a tornado was going to hit a town in Kansas and alerted a railroad company in that town. The railroad stopped two trains heading toward town, and "the crews watched as the massive tornado, illuminated by lightning, passed between them."[92]

Welcome to the world of "open data," the idea that institutions like governments should make data publicly available, free to reuse, and easy for computers to analyze.[93] Besides the weather industry, open data has made, and can make, a tremendous economic impact. For instance, in 1983 the US government made GPS data publicly available — and today over 3 million jobs, from truck driving to precision farming, rely on open GPS data.[94] (Self-driving cars do, too.[95])

As if that wasn't enough, McKinsey estimated that government open data could unleash $3 trillion a year in economic activity.[96] For example, open transportation data could help companies find optimal shipping routes, and open pricing data could help companies decide how much to pay contractors.[97]

Open data can also have widespread social benefits. Open data can help citizens hold government accountable, like when a team of journalists used government purchasing data released by the Ukrainian government to identify widespread instances of corruption, like when a hospital bought 50 mops from a mysterious company for 75 British pounds each.[98] It can also help citizens and companies make useful apps: for instance, in 2013 Yelp integrated open restaurant inspection scores from San Francisco and New York into its app so that Yelp users could see restaurants' hygiene ratings.[99] And it can lead to massive cost savings: a British researcher found that one public dataset could help the UK's National Health Service save hundreds of millions of pounds.[100]

Clearly, open data has tremendous potential. So how do we get some?

The policy and politics of open data

Unfortunately, you can't just wave a wand and make governments release their data. Many bureaucracies are slow to adopt technology or hesitant to release information that could make them look bad.[101] Thankfully, many governments have started taking the initiative. The UK government signed the Open Data Charter in 2013, which made its agencies commit to publishing their data by default.[102]

The US followed suit with the 2013 Open Data Policy, which required all new agency data to be released publicly on a website called data.gov.[103] Data.gov contains free data on everything from college tuition to agriculture to consumer complaints against big businesses.[104] And in 2014, the American government mandated that all spending data be made public at usaspending.gov with the Digital Accountability and Transparency Act (known as the DATA Act).[105] Cities like San Francisco[106] and Boston[107] followed suit and created their own open data portals, as did countries like Canada[108] and Japan.[109]

These policies haven't been free from bureaucratic pushback, however. The UK's government agencies, for instance, were initially reluctant to go through the work of opening their data without evidence for why open data would be in their own best interest.[110] And open data is very much vulnerable to shifting political attitudes. While the UK became the world's open data leader by 2015,[111] open data advocates feared in 2016 that Brexit would threaten Britain's growing open data culture.

They feared that austerity measures could make government agencies stop spending the money required to publish and maintain open datasets, never mind the fact that the political drama around Brexit could have distracted from the open data push.[112]

Level	Format
★	Make your data available on the web (in any format)
★★	Make it available as structured data (for example, Microsoft Excel instead of image scan of a table)
★★★	Make it available in an open, non-proprietary format (for example, CSV or XML instead of Microsoft Excel)
★★★★	In addition to using open formats, use Uniform Resource Locators (URLs) to identify things using open standards and recommendations from W3C, so that other people can point at your stuff
★★★★★	In addition to using open formats and using URLs to identify things, link your data to other people's data to provide context

Sir Tim Berners-Lee, the creator of the internet, argued that there are five levels of open data, as shown in this chart. Governments should aspire to reach the highest possible level. Source: UK Parliament[113]

There are some legitimate policy debates around open data, as well. Governments can't just publish everything; they need to ensure that the data they publish doesn't compromise privacy or national security.[114] Sometimes, data releases could unintentionally be used to hurt citizens. For instance, the Help America Vote Act of 2002 required all 50 states and DC to maintain a central database of all registered voters,[115] which contains information including voters' names, ages, and addresses.[116] Many states started selling this data to residents;[117] political candidates[118] and researchers[119] found this information particularly valuable. But Neel, one of the authors of this book, ran a study that found that criminals could combine public voter rolls with Airbnb listing information to figure out the exact names and addresses of millions of Airbnb hosts.[120] Governments need to be more careful when deciding what personal data to publish.

In short, open data has tremendous potential, and governments have good reason to expand the range of data they release. But policymakers also need to work with companies and citizens to address issues of privacy and security.[121]

How could companies be held liable for data breaches?

When companies make mistakes that harm people, they're usually held accountable. When BP's *Deepwater Horizon* oil rig exploded in the Gulf of Mexico in 2010, causing mass devastation to the nearby environment, BP had to pay $18.7 billion in penalties to the US government.[122] After the American company Enron collapsed due to fraud, it had to pay $7.2 billion in settlements to shareholders who lost money.[123]

Companies have started facing a new threat: data breaches. For instance, hackers leaked the names, email addresses, birthdays, and telephone numbers of one billion Yahoo users in 2016.[124] And in 2017, hackers attacked the American credit bureau Equifax, stealing the Social Security numbers of 143 million users — more than half the US's adult population.[125]

The problem? Unlike BP or Enron, companies who suffer data breaches don't often get punished, and affected consumers don't usually get compensated. For instance, after the health insurance giant Anthem was hacked and leaked the information of 80 million accounts, customers filed a class-action lawsuit but got under $1 apiece.[126] As one frustrated pundit put it after the Equifax breach:

> I don't doubt that companies regret these things, but I don't think they care that much either. To them it means just a few days of bad press and at most a fine that amounts to a minuscule portion of their profits. With penalties like that, why would companies bother to make things better?[127]

Experts are calling for companies to be held more liable for data breaches,[128] and that's beginning to happen — in a few countries, at least. In 2016, the EU created a landmark law called the General Data Protection Regulation (GDPR).[129] Under this law, companies who are breached have to pay fines of up to 20 million Euros or 4% of their annual revenue, whichever is more.[130] The UK passed a similar law called the Data Protection Act, which requires that companies keep your data "safe and secure" and "for no longer than is absolutely necessary."[131]

The US, meanwhile, has much lighter data protection and privacy laws.[132] While Congress has made some pro-data protection rules, it hasn't gone very far. For instance, in 2014 Congress proposed the Data Breach and Notification Act, which would require companies to notify customers after a breach, offer free credit monitoring to customers affected by a breach, and report large breaches to the government.[133] But the bill never even made it to a vote.[134] It's a start, though.

Data protection laws vary significantly between countries, and especially between the US and EU. Experts have called for "transatlantic data charters," where American and European regulators would set common policies for how companies should store, share, and protect their data.[135] Unfortunately, past US-EU talks on this topic have gotten bogged down by widespread disagreements.[136]

But if both sides of the Atlantic can finally agree, international companies will be spared the confusion and hassle that comes with having to obey multiple, often conflicting, data protection laws.[137] This transatlantic data charter would be especially helpful to smaller companies; currently, huge companies can easily hire armies of lawyers to sort through the many burdensome data protection laws, but startups without those resources are out of luck.

As data protection laws spread, some insurance companies are starting to offer data breach insurance.[138] Like with normal health and auto insurance, companies would pay a small amount every year, and in exchange the insurer would cover the costs if a devastating data breach happens.[139]

Let's go back to the original question: how could companies be held liable for data breaches? Well, policymakers could allow — or even enforce — strict penalties like the ones seen in Europe; they could also require some form of data insurance for companies that hold sensitive data. But until then, American consumers' data continues to be at risk.

Chapter 12.
Trends Going Forward

Few fields change as quickly as technology. We can't claim to see the future, but we can lift the veil on some up-and-coming technologies and show what we think the world might look like in the coming years. In this final chapter, let's look to the future and see what we can learn.

What's the future of self-driving cars?

Imagine a world with no traffic jams as a steady stream of cars chugs down the highway.[1] In this world, there would be 90% fewer accidents than today,[2] we wouldn't need giant parking lots,[3] and you could spend your commute eating a sit-down meal or taking a nap.[4]

This is, of course, the vision of the world if self-driving cars become the dominant form of transportation. Ever since Google started testing prototypes of its self-driving cars on the streets of Mountain View, California in 2015,[5] these autonomous vehicles (AVs) have captured people's imaginations.

So what's going to happen with self-driving cars?

Under the hood

First off, let's explore how a car can drive itself. A self-driving car needs two things: information about its environment and a strategy for how to move through it.[6]

Self-driving cars come with a huge collection of sensors and data to understand where the car is and what's around it. A self-driving car uses GPS,[7] speedometer-like sensors called "inertial navigation systems,"[8] and maps to figure out where it is.[9]

Once the car knows where it is, it needs to build an exact model of what's around it: cars, pedestrians, street signs, and more.[10] To build this model, the car starts with maps to figure out the landscape. These aren't your garden-variety Google Maps, though; they're precise to the inch and include features like the height of every curb and the position of every traffic sign.[11]

A self-driving car prototype made by Google's affiliate Waymo. Source: Wikimedia[12]

Then, to figure out objects on the road, the car uses a spinning laser mounted on top of the car, called LIDAR, to create a 360° model of its surroundings. But LIDAR only tells the car that there are obstacles around; it can't tell the obstacles apart. For that, the car uses onboard cameras.[13] Ultimately, the car builds a 3D model of the world, including the landscape and objects around it.[14]

Then the car has to make a driving strategy. Based on its current speed and position, the car computes a large set of possible actions, or "short-range plans," for how it could get closer to its destination: change lanes, make a turn, accelerate, and so on. Then it removes plans that would bring it too close to an obstacle, and it ranks the remaining plans by safety and speed. Once the car chooses the best plan, it sends those instructions to the wheels, brake, and "gas pedal" to make the car move. All of this computation happens within 50 milliseconds.[15]

The learning car

It's important to note that it's impossible to teach a car all the rules of driving. You can embed some basic rules, like "green means go," but you can't embed every single rule because there are too many unique situations the car could be in (like if the car is on a 3-lane highway in a slight drizzle and a 14-foot car going 43 mph tries merging in).

Instead, developers teach the car how to learn driving by identifying patterns. For instance, suppose the car notices that, when bicyclists extend their left arm, they turn left 90% of the time — the car could then infer that the left arm is bicyclists' left turn signal and start slowing down when it sees it in the future. Thus, the car learns how to avoid cyclists without any human telling it what to do (the car might not even know what a cyclist is).[16] This is machine learning at its simplest: a computer making predictions based on observed patterns.[17]

Taxis vs. Pods

The technology for self-driving cars is getting there, so it's only a matter of time before they go mainstream. There are two competing visions for how self-driving cars will first go mainstream — we call them the "taxi" vision and the "pod" vision — and several companies are duking it out in each arena.

Companies in the "taxi" arena think self-driving cars' path forward looks a lot like Uber: a fleet of electric, self-driving cars patrols nonstop around a city, shuttling passengers around and never stopping to park. Everyone rides in self-driving cars, but nobody owns their own car.[18]

In this arena are ridesharing companies like Uber, which is working hard on self-driving taxis.[19] Lyft has partnered with Waymo to combine the companies' core talents — making a ridesharing network and creating the tech to power cars — with the hope of launching autonomous taxis as well.[20] Waymo also launched its own autonomous taxi service, called Waymo One, in Phoenix in 2018.[21]

Conventional car manufacturers are also fighting for this space, and many are partnering with software startups to give their cars the self-driving chops they need. Ford invested $1 billion in the self-driving software startup Argo AI in 2017,[22] and the year before GM bought a similar startup called Cruise Automation.[23]

The self-driving taxi world won't be won on self-driving tech alone. Waymo One, for instance, has a tremendous advantage thanks to its affiliation with Google. Google Maps has a ridesharing tab, which shows users the prices of Uber, Lyft, and other local apps.[24] Many people probably go straight to this tab to compare ridesharing options — so Google could theoretically siphon riders away from Uber and Lyft by promoting Waymo One in this tab and sidelining rival apps. If even a fraction of Google Maps' one billion users[25] jumped to Waymo One, Uber and Lyft would be in serious trouble. And, in theory, Google could make Uber and Lyft's lives even harder by restricting access to Google Maps APIs (which, if you recall, the Uber and Lyft apps use heavily).

A strange-looking self-driving "pod" that shuttled Londoners along a fixed route in the Greenwich neighborhood. This was an experiment to see if slow-moving shuttles in tightly-defined areas are viable. Source: Wikimedia[26]

In the "pod" arena are companies that think it'll take too long for self-driving cars to get to the point where humans can ride them on highways; self-driving car prototypes have long struggled with the high speeds and merging of highways.[27] Instead, many startups are betting that self-driving cars will see their first successes in slow, low-risk applications,[28] usually going no more than 25mph.[29] Many of these "cars" — like the pictured self-driving London shuttle[30] — don't look much like cars at all.[31]

Startups in the "pod" world have found some creative use cases. May Mobility creates self-driving pods that shuttle employees around corporate campuses.[32] The startup Nuro figured that, while self-driving cars aren't yet safe enough to shuttle humans around at high speeds, they're perfectly fine for delivering groceries; Nuro's delivery pods have launched successfully in Phoenix.[33] These companies are betting that they can quickly master this limited use case of self-driving cars and learn enough that they can beat the Ubers and Waymos of the world in more advanced use cases.[34]

Amazon is a particularly interesting case because it's looking into both potential futures for self-driving cars. On one hand, it's considering jumping into self-driving taxis. If Amazon partnered with Lyft on self-driving taxis, as some analysts think it might, Amazon could offer steep discounts to Prime members and beat out Uber.[35] On the pod side, Amazon is also reportedly considering building out a self-driving delivery network to ship Prime packages even faster.[36] (It could even do both, with driverless pods shuttling people and packages around to maximize efficiency.)

None of these technologies have moved past the testing phase yet, but that's likely to change in the coming years.

Speed bumps

The last thing we'll mention is that self-driving cars have some significant challenges facing them before they can go mainstream.

One is technological; self-driving cars still have safety issues. A Tesla in its self-driving "autopilot" mode was blamed for a man's death in 2016,[37] and a self-driving Uber killed a woman in Arizona in 2018.[38]

Second is legal. India banned self-driving cars in 2017 to protect driving jobs,[39] Europe has been notoriously slow in allowing testing of self-driving cars,[40] and even in the US only a few cities have allowed testing so far.[41]

Third, and perhaps hardest, is ethical problems. What should a self-driving car do if it has to choose between injuring its driver or a pedestrian?[42] If self-driving car company programs its cars to make a decision, is the car programmed to kill?[43] To bring transparency to these ethical dilemmas, philosophers and technologists have called for "algorithmic transparency": the principle that self-driving cars' algorithms be made public.[44]

Are robots going to take our jobs?

Manufacturing robots have already put thousands of industrial workers out of a job, leading to an uptick in poverty.[45] A report issued in 2015 was even more grim: it predicted that automation would kill over 4.6 million office and administrative jobs by 2020.[46] In other words, both skilled and unskilled workers seem to be in trouble. It seems that robots will inevitably take our jobs.

Or will they?

The economics of tech and labor

Economists group technologies into two categories: labor-enabling and labor-replacing. Labor-enabling technologies help workers be more productive. For example, consider PCs and the internet — they've made it far easier to write essays, find information, or talk to coworkers. Then there are labor-replacing technologies, like the self-driving cars and industrial robots we mentioned before. As the name implies, labor-replacing technologies can remove the need for human workers. These opposing forces are in a constant tug-of-war.[47]

Who wins? The results might be unexpected. For instance, think about the ATM, which became popular in the 1970s. Most customers no longer needed to talk to a teller inside a bank's branch office. Many people assumed that this would eliminate the teller job altogether. Right? Wrong.[48]

Thanks to the ATM, banks needed fewer human tellers in their branches. But this made branches cheaper to operate, which led to banks opening more branches. And that, in turn, led banks to employ more tellers. The upshot? The number of tellers in the US grew from 300,000 to 600,000 from 1970 to 2010.[49] In other words, the ATM actually *created* teller jobs instead of replacing them.

So what does this mean for us in the age of artificial intelligence and robots?

The case for and against job theft

There's pretty strong evidence that automation will take away lots of jobs. A 2013 Oxford study found that half of all American jobs were at risk of automation by 2033.[50] People with lower skill levels would be particularly hurt. President Obama's Chief Economic Adviser found that 83% of jobs paying under $20 an hour were at risk of automation, versus just 4% of jobs making over $40 an hour.[51] Furthermore, 44% of jobs requiring less than a high school education were likely to be automated, compared to just 1% of jobs requiring a bachelor's degree.[52] In other words, robots could take our jobs, and it'd especially hurt the least educated and most vulnerable.

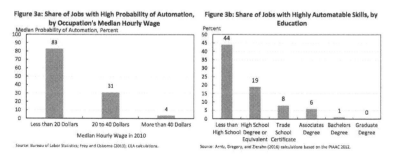

A 2016 report showed that people with lower-paying jobs, fewer skills, and less education were more at risk of losing their jobs to automation.
Source: *Council of Economic Advisors*[53]

But there's also data to indicate that robots *aren't* taking our jobs. Throughout the mid-2010s, American unemployment was low (less than 5% in 2017), workers were staying at their jobs longer, and wages were slightly rising.[54] That hardly indicates that robots are massively stealing jobs.

More broadly, automation could move people away from doing more manual tasks to doing more tasks that require the human mind. For instance, manufacturing plants envision having fewer assembly-line workers in the future — but more engineers, coders, and managers.[55] Technology has created entire industries, like IT and software development.[56] Automation wouldn't just create science, technology, engineering, and math (STEM) jobs, either: self-driving cars will still need mechanics and marketers, for instance.[57]

So what's the verdict? No one can agree. Pundits are split — sometimes hilariously so. For instance, one writer penned a New York Times piece saying, "The Long-Term Jobs Killer Is Not China. It's Automation."[58] But a Wired writer said, "[T]he answer is very clearly not automation, it's China." [59]

Haves and have-nots

Most scholars believe that high-skill workers will have a lot to gain from automation, while low-skilled workers will have more to lose.[60] In other words, the poor would get poorer while the rich would get richer.

One way to mitigate this problem is education. There will be plenty of new jobs available but, unless something changes, there won't be enough skilled workers to fill them. In 2015,

Deloitte estimated that manufacturing would add 3.5 million jobs by 2025 thanks to automation — but 2 million of those would go unfilled due to a lack of skilled workers.[61] Proposals to combat this include apprenticeships to help people pick up skills on the job, investment in vocational education at community colleges, and promoting STEM education in high school and college.[62]

Some more radical suggestions have been proposed. Elon Musk projected that automation could send unemployment up to 30-40% (again, no one agrees on the impact of automation), so he proposed a "universal basic income." Under this scheme, governments would send every resident a check, which he said would fight poverty and protect the economy from certain collapse. Musk's universal basic income would be funded by a government tax on robots.[63]

As it happens, Bill Gates has long had a proposal to tax robots — or rather, to tax the companies that employ robots. Proponents say the revenue could fund jobs that humans are uniquely good at, like childcare.[64]

White-collar risk?

Some scholars take the opposite approach, arguing that white-collar jobs are as endangered as blue-collar jobs, if not more so. The writer Kai-Fu Lee argues that there's not much economic incentive to automate low-skill, low-wage jobs like baristas; instead, companies looking to save money would rather eliminate skilled, high-paying jobs like financial analysts.[65]

There have indeed been a few notable cases when artificial intelligence has managed to match professional humans' job performance. An AI bot called Amelia has proved surprisingly good at customer support for banks, insurers, and telecom companies; she uses humanlike facial expressions and gestures and tries to empathize with callers. And with every customer she handles, she gets even better.[66]

Even higher-skill jobs have been getting automated. One Japanese insurance company replaced 34 human agents with IBM's Watson AI, and large numbers of people in the mortgage financing industry have seen their jobs get destroyed by automation.[67] AI can't yet replace doctors and lawyers, but some AIs have gotten good at the kind of research paralegals often do, and robots can now do some medical operations — both at a fraction of the cost of their human counterparts.[68]

How could you make video and audio "fake news"?

In 2017, a Canadian company called Lyrebird published audio of Donald Trump, Barack Obama, and Hillary Clinton reading their Tweets aloud.[69] There was just one problem: none of them had actually read their Tweets — the audio was faked![70]

Thanks to a new technology, you can create convincing but fake video and audio in a fraction of the time it would take you to manually imitate it.[71] In this era of fake news, many people have stopped believing news they hear online, relying on video or audio to confirm that something really happened. But if video and audio can also be faked, we wouldn't have anything left to trust.[72] So how can you make fake video and audio footage?

These "deepfakes" are generated by a mysterious technology called "generative adversarial networks," or GANs. GANs are a special version of a technology called neural networks.[73] So before we explain how GANs work, let's look at neural networks.

Neural networks

Your brain learns things by experimenting, getting feedback, and adjusting.[74] For instance, say you're new to baking and want to bake a cake. You throw together a random mix of flour, sugar, eggs, butter, and other ingredients, toss the batter in the oven for a random amount of time, and see how it turns out. A friend tastes the cake and gives you comments: too sweet, undercooked, needs more chocolate. You slightly adjust your recipe to address the comments, and while your friend might be happier, they still have suggestions. Repeat this process, and eventually you'll have tweaked your approach enough to become a master cake baker — without ever picking up a cookbook. You learn this way because your brain contains a "neural network":[75] a collection of connected cells called neurons that talk to each other.[76]

To make computers more powerful, computer scientists have tried to simulate your brain's neural network inside a computer. It's called an "artificial neural network," but many technologists (somewhat confusingly) just call it a "neural network."[77] Like the cake example, an artificial neural network keeps track of many variables and assigns each variable a "weight": the amount of butter, the time to bake, or the oven temperature, to name a few.[78] As you give the artificial neural network feedback, it tweaks the weights to get closer to the right answer, much like you adjusted your cake recipe based on your friend's feedback.[79]

Neural networks are incredibly powerful: they can autocorrect text on your phone, catch spam emails, translate languages, or read your handwriting, among many other things.[80] Neural networks are great at recognizing things, but they aren't designed to generate new stuff, like fake audio and video.[81] For that, let's turn to an even stronger variation of neural networks.

Generative adversarial networks

In a "generative adversarial network," or GAN, you create two neural networks and make them face off. The "generator" network tries to make something fake, and the "discriminator" guesses whether or not the generator's creation is real or not.[82]

The networks get into a sort of arms race, with the generator trying to make more convincing forgeries and the discriminator trying to get better at policing fakes.[83] The networks learn from each other, constantly improving, until the generator is churning out incredibly convincing fake things.[84]

As an example, imagine you want to make a generative adversarial network that creates a fake video of an American CEO giving a speech. You create the generator and discriminator network. Originally, neither network has any idea what it's doing, so the generator might make a video of a person speaking Italian, and the discriminator won't know that it's fake. So you step in and show the discriminator a real video of an American CEO speaking. From the video, the discriminator learns that American CEOs usually speak English. So the discriminator starts rejecting videos of people speaking other languages. The generator picks up on this, so it starts trying different languages to trick the discriminator. Eventually the generator discovers that videos of a person speaking English pass the discriminator. This back-and-forth continues until the generator can make convincing fake videos.[85]

So, what would we do if we started seeing faked videos of presidential candidates giving inflammatory speeches?[86] No clue — but at least we'd know how the fakers made the videos.

Why did Facebook buy a company that makes virtual reality headsets?

Facebook shocked the tech world when, in 2014, it acquired the makers of a virtual reality (VR) headset called the Oculus Rift, which was mostly used for video games.[87] It initially seemed strange that this social media company would buy this gaming company.[88]

The purchase didn't make much immediate financial sense either. VR has had a sluggish consumer debut,[89] as evidenced by the Oculus Rift's repeated price cuts since its launch.[90] Instead, Facebook CEO Mark Zuckerberg admitted the purchase was a long-term ploy, saying in 2016 it would take another 10 years for VR to reach mass market.[91]

Facebook imagined that virtual reality would be the future of communication.[92] Instead of just connecting over text, images, or videos, Zuckerberg explained a future where you could use VR to experience sports games, university lectures, appointments with doctors, and adventures with friends, all from the comfort of your home.[93] (Critics said that seemed a bit far-fetched, since strapping on a heavy, expensive headset just to chat with friends might get tiring after a while.[94] However, Facebook is optimistic that VR headsets will one day be as slim as Ray-Bans.[95])

If Zuckerberg is right, owning the socially-focused Oculus Rift headset could be valuable for Facebook. Facebook's strategy has long been to maximize the time people spend on its platforms;[96] more time equals more chances to show ads and more user data to make the ads better-targeted.[97] Facebook could try to get users to spend lots of time on the Oculus Rift, at which point Facebook could start sliding in engaging new forms of advertising: product placement, game-like ads, or immersive ads for concerts, to name a few ideas.[98]

For evidence of this theory, consider how Facebook started letting Oculus Rift owners stream live VR videos to their Facebook timelines in 2017.[99] Oculus Rift owners could start hanging out around a table in VR, doing things like answering audience questions (avatars can "grab" posters containing audience comments), chatting, or doodling in the air.[100]

An example of a VR live video on Facebook: virtual office hours with a professor. Source: Facebook[101]

This new feature is a clever way to build buzz around virtual reality,[102] which could encourage curious viewers to buy headsets.

So why did Facebook acquire a virtual reality headset company? It's not just for video games. Facebook sees VR as the future of computing and social networking, and they want to be a leader in that space.[103]

Why are so many companies afraid of Amazon?

In 2018, Amazon acquired the drug distribution startup PillPack, which was licensed to send American customers medications through the mail.[104] The pharmacy industry panicked, and their stock prices tanked as investors fled: Rite Aid fell 11%, Walgreens fell 10%, and CVS fell 6% overnight.[105]

There are very few companies so feared that they can send companies' stocks tumbling just by making preliminary moves into their industries. Analysts say that no sector is safe from Amazon,[106] a company that has ravaged everything from books to groceries to movies to hardware.[107] How is Amazon so powerful, and what might it do next?

Terrifying tech

Amazon's vast reserves of money have enabled it to start encroaching into other major tech companies' personal space, which has made them nervous.

One thing to worry Google is that Amazon has become many shoppers' preferred search engine; more than half of product searches start on Amazon.[108] This means many companies are starting to move ad dollars toward Amazon because that's where their consumers are. Plus, with Alexa being the biggest voice computing platform, more and more customers can just ask Alexa to buy something — bypassing Google and web browsers entirely.[109]

Facebook is also threatened by Amazon's expansion into video streaming and social media, which it kicked off by buying the video game live streaming service Twitch in 2014.[110] Since the acquisition, though, Twitch has grown into live streaming talk shows, music, podcasts, workouts, and more,[111] coming into direct competition with Facebook's live streaming service, Facebook Live.[112] Amazon Prime Video is also taking on Facebook Watch for the movies market. And Amazon's growth into ads scared Facebook so much that, in 2019, Facebook started officially listing Amazon as a competitor in its annual filing with the Securities and Exchange Commission (SEC).[113]

Amazon is also threatening Apple's precious hardware and voice services. Siri was the first major voice assistant, but Alexa has since gained more market share than her.[114] Apple has traditionally been the leader in smart gadgets, but Amazon has released huge numbers of its own Alexa-powered gadgets: Echo speakers, smart microwaves, wall clocks, car accessories, and many more.[115] In 2017, entertainment pundits started murmuring that the Echo brand was becoming cooler than Apple — bad news for Apple, which lives and dies by its brand name.[116]

Finally, Microsoft went all-in on cloud computing once Satya Nadella took the reins as CEO in 2014, focusing its resources on its Azure division.[117] But Amazon Web Services (AWS) still has more customers than Azure and rakes in more money.[118]

Ads, social media, hardware, and cloud — Azure hits them all, and it has its rivals quaking in their boots. But, at this point, Amazon is much more than a tech company.

Retail & beyond

Amazon is famously ruthless when it tries to expand its e-commerce empire. In 2009, Amazon noticed an up-and-coming online retail startup called Quidsi, which sold baby products on Diapers.com. Amazon sent an executive to have lunch with the Quidsi founders and offered to buy the company. The founders said no.[119] But then Amazon started aggressively undercutting Diapers.com's prices[120] and rolling out a competing "Amazon Mom" program. It cost Amazon millions, but it ruined Quidsi, which was eventually forced to sell to Amazon at a steep discount.[121]

So it wasn't all that surprising when Amazon aggressively entered the grocery market by buying Whole Foods in 2017 — which made the grocery chain Kroger's stocks tumble 8% overnight.[122] (Notice a pattern?)

Amazon, long famous for killing off bookstores, has started its own.
Source: Shinya Suzuki[123]

But retail isn't enough: Amazon has started making big moves into the healthcare space as well. The PillPack purchase, for instance, removed one of pharmacies' last defensible advantages: the legal ability to sell prescription medications.[124] (Now you can buy pills online with your cereal and charging cables.)

Amazon has also started a line of home health products,[125] explored kits to let consumers run health tests at home,[126] and filed a patent for Alexa to notice colds or coughs.[127] Put this together and you can envision a future where Alexa notices you're sick, Amazon mails you a health test kit, you send it back, a virtual doctor prescribes medication, and PillPack mails you the pills.[128]

In 2018, Amazon launched its biggest attack on the healthcare space yet by partnering with JPMorgan and Berkshire Hathaway to "reduce wasteful spending" in healthcare and "cut out middlemen."[129] We think that's coded language for aggressively using AI and other new technologies to replace doctors, pharmacists, and insurance agents. Because Amazon doesn't employ anybody who would lose their jobs as a result of this initiative, it can freely try to burn down the whole industry and remake it in its image.

Core competencies

So why is Amazon so good in virtually every industry it gets into? The answer: Amazon isn't a tech company or a cloud company or a diapers or books or healthcare company. It's an infrastructure company.[130]

Amazon's decades of success in e-commerce has led it to build up hundreds of strategically-placed warehouses,[131] titanic distribution centers staffed with tens of thousands of workers,[132] and a ground and air transportation network that can compete with FedEx or UPS.[133] Overall, this logistics network is second to none.[134]

Amazon's network's one weakness was fresh food, which can't be stored for a long time or shipped extremely long distances the same way a book can.[135] But Amazon patched that up with its Whole Foods purchase:[136] Whole Foods' 400 mostly-urban locations instantly became 400 warehouses from which Amazon could quickly ship fresh food to urban customers.[137]

So Amazon's expertise in warehousing and delivery infrastructure makes it easy for Amazon to sell any new type of goods it gets its hands on — like pills. What's more, because Amazon is a digital company and not a brick-and-mortar company, it can scale up quickly and cheaply; it just needs to add a bit more to its website and grow its logistics network a bit. Meanwhile, even the mighty Walmart needs to spend $37 million to open a new store.[138]

Amazon's skill with infrastructure goes beyond physical goods, though. The dominance of Amazon Web Services shows just how good Amazon's *digital* infrastructure is: servers, data centers, and the like.[139]

In short, Amazon's mastery of the supply chain lets it grow quickly in any market it tries to enter. And, with each additional market it enters and each additional product it launches,

Amazon gains even more data, which it can use to further fuel its growth.[140]

Antitrust action?

As Amazon has grown from an online bookstore to an all-encompassing powerhouse, it's no surprise that people have started taking aim. People have started protesting against Amazon's ability to bend companies and governments to its will,[141] and many have argued that Amazon has grown monopolistic and needs to be broken up.[142]

The case for breaking up Amazon is pretty clear. It's had a long history of anticompetitive behavior. It's had a history of undercutting competitors — just remember the Diapers.com saga[143] — and, after the Whole Foods purchase, Amazon was attacked for blocking any future grocery delivery startups from entering the market at all.[144] And Amazon has been the poster child for the trend of American vertical mergers[145] as it's brought voice assistants, shopping, cloud computing, and media under one roof.[146]

In short, it's clear that Amazon displays monopolistic tendencies. The problem is that US antitrust laws are primarily designed to prevent horizontal mergers, or when head-to-head competitors try to merge — like when the US blocked the ISP giants Comcast and Time Warner Cable from merging in 2015.[147] So, for antitrust regulation against Amazon to succeed, it would have to argue that Amazon's vertical integration has stifled innovation and unfairly tilted the playing field.[148]

If Amazon *does* get split up, AWS is the most likely piece to go. AWS serves very different people and has a very different business structure from Amazon's core business — which is retail, Prime, and Alexa — so it would make the most sense as its own company.[149] In fact, AWS might even do better alone when you consider that "pure-play" cloud companies have historically grown far faster than companies with a mix of cloud and other business units.[150] (Meanwhile, Microsoft Azure, Google Cloud, IBM Cloud, and all of AWS's other competitors are all bundled with a variety of unrelated, and slower-growing, business units — Azure might be Microsoft's main focus, but it's far from their only product.) For these reasons, we wouldn't be surprised to see AWS get spun off proactively!

But, even without AWS, Amazon would probably continue to terrify companies across the world just fine.

Conclusion

You're never done learning — about tech or about anything else — but you've certainly finished the main content of *Swipe to Unlock*.

We think the case studies and analysis we've provided will leave you with a stronger understanding of the *what* and the *why* behind technology. We hope you'll be better prepared to launch the next great app, shape your company's business strategy, or make sense of the next big tech news story.

Before you go, we have a few last things to cover.

Reference material

Now that you've read the main content, we hope *Swipe to Unlock* will become a useful reference for you going forward.

To that end, we've included a glossary after this chapter. There, we've defined dozens of technology and business terms, including some we didn't get time to cover in the meat of this book, like explanations of popular programming languages, business acronyms, and the types of employees at tech companies.

We've also included an index where you can look up companies, products, concepts, and people. If you're interviewing at a tech company, for instance, you could look up the company and read the key sections about the company's strategy and products.

Want to take your resume to the next level?

If you're looking for a new job, we hope what you've learned from *Swipe to Unlock* will be valuable. But to show potential employers what you know, you have to get the interview first.

The three of us successfully navigated the Google, Facebook, and Microsoft recruiting processes, so we've learned what can make your resume stand out from the pack. **We've distilled our knowledge into a 30-page guide to help you craft a great resume and get more interviews** in consulting, product management, marketing, or anything in between.

We usually sell our resume guide to career consulting clients for $99, but if you share what you liked about *Swipe to* Unlock in an Amazon review, we'll give you a copy for free.

Just email a screenshot of your "Verified Purchase" review to team@swipetounlock.com to get your free copy of our ultimate resume guide!

Check out our second book, *Bubble or Revolution*!

Since we wrote *Swipe to Unlock*, no technologies have made as big a splash as blockchains and cryptocurrencies. But nobody is quite sure what to make of them: some call them scams, some call them the "biggest invention since the internet."

Our second book, *Bubble or Revolution*, breaks down the core concepts of blockchains and cryptocurrencies and offers a balanced, comprehensive, and accessible analysis of their strengths, weaknesses, and future potential. Nir Eyal, the bestselling author of *Hooked*, called it "a brilliant overview of what could the next big thing in tech, authored by leaders at today's top tech companies."

Bubble or Revolution is now available on Amazon (swipetounlock.com/bubble) and Barnes & Noble. Get your copy today!

Want us to speak at your company, conference, or university?

If you enjoyed *Swipe to Unlock* and want us to speak at your organization's event, email speaking@swipetounlock.com with details about your event and the approximate dates. We always love meeting our readers in person and discussing technology and business strategy!

Neel Mehta, Product Manager at Google

Adi Agashe, Product Manager at Microsoft

Parth Detroja, Product Manager at Facebook

Stay in touch

To hear about our predictions for the tech industry, analysis of current tech events, and tips for breaking into the tech industry, follow us on LinkedIn!

You'll find us on LinkedIn at:
- linkedin.com/in/neelmehta18
- linkedin.com/in/adityaagashe
- linkedin.com/in/parthdetroja

If you share a photo of your copy of *Swipe to Unlock* on LinkedIn and tag the three of us (Neel Mehta, Aditya Agashe, and Parth Detroja), we'll all connect with you and like, comment on, or share your post to help you get more views and followers.

Thank you!

We hope you've enjoyed *Swipe to Unlock* and that what you've learned here is useful for your life and career. Writing this book has been a lot of fun for us, so we're glad you joined us for the ride. If you found *Swipe to Unlock* useful, we hope you'll review it on Amazon and recommend it to your friends.

Thank you for reading, and until next time, all the best!

— Neel, Adi, and Parth

Glossary

So how do you build a website? Just ask your average tech blog, and it'll tell you: open a GitHub repo; build out a backend in Python or Ruby on Rails; serve up some HTML, CSS, and JavaScript; build some RESTful APIs; tweak the UI/UX; and ship an MVP on AWS. Oh, and get a CDN while you're at it.

Huh?

The world of software has a mind-boggling amount of jargon and buzzwords. But here, we're going to break down some of the most common terms so you can talk like a techie without feeling like you need a foreign language class.

Programming languages

All software is written using code, much like food is made according to a recipe. And just like you can write recipes in English, Bengali, or Turkish, you can write software in programming languages like Ruby, Python, or C. Each programming language has its own strengths and weaknesses, and each one is used in particular situations. Here's a glimpse into some of the most popular languages.

Assembly

Computers only think in 1's and 0's, and assembly language is just a slightly prettier version of 1's and 0's. Programmers rarely write in assembly language, since it's too much effort; they'll usually write in a "higher-level language" that computers convert into assembly and then run. (Every other language in this section is a higher-level, or more "abstract," language.) It's like driving a car: instead of trying to directly set the speed of each wheel, you just use the steering wheel and pedals. This is far easier, and besides, you'd probably have no idea how to set the wheel speeds just right.

C/C++

Some of the oldest programming languages, and still among the most popular. They run very fast but are more difficult to write, so developers trying to get maximum performance (like those writing graphics-heavy games, physics simulators, web servers, or operating systems) tend to use C and C++.

C# (C-Sharp)

A language built by Microsoft, often used to write desktop apps. Similar to Java.

CSS

A web development language that works with HTML, used to make websites look pretty. CSS lets you change a webpage's colors, fonts, background, and so on. It also lets you specify where the various buttons, headers, images, etc. on a webpage should go.

Go

An up-and-coming language designed by Google, often used to build web servers.

HTML

The language used to write webpages. You can create links, images, headers, buttons, and every other element on a webpage using HTML. Each of these elements is called a "tag." For instance, a tag called <img> represents an image.

Java

One of the world's most popular languages, Java is used to write Android apps, web servers, and desktop apps. It's famous for its "write once, run anywhere" tagline — the same Java app can instantly run on all kinds of devices.[1]

JavaScript

The language used to make webpages interactive. Every web app you use, from Facebook Messenger to Spotify to Google Maps, uses JavaScript. Nowadays, developers also use JavaScript to build web servers and desktop apps. *Also known as ECMAScript or ES.*

MATLAB

A specialized, commercial language that's often used in engineering, science, and mathematical modeling. It's used more for research than building software.

Objective-C

A language formerly used to write iPhone, iPad, and Mac apps; nowadays, people tend to develop in Swift.

PHP

A language used to write web servers. It's fallen out of favor among developers in recent years, but Facebook is still written using a custom "dialect" of PHP.[2]

Python

A popular, easy-to-learn language that's common in introductory computer science courses. It's widely used for data science and writing web servers.

R

A data analysis language, which lets you graph, summarize, and interpret huge amounts of data.

Ruby

A language often used for building web apps through the popular web-server software Ruby on Rails.

SQL

Structured Query Language: a language for working with databases. Like Excel, it lets you work with tables, rows, and columns. You can run "queries" to filter, sort, combine, and analyze the data.

Swift

Apple's language used for writing iPhone, iPad, and Mac apps. Replaced Objective-C.

TypeScript

Microsoft's expanded version of JavaScript, which adds extra features to make building large apps easier. Browsers can't run TypeScript directly, so you use a tool to "transcompile" or "transpile" it to JavaScript first.

Data

We humans like storing information in Excel files or Word documents. Computers, however, prefer storing data in simple text files. Here are a few popular ways to store data in a "machine-readable" format.

CSV

Comma-separated values: a way to store data in lightweight tables, similar to an Excel file but much simpler. These files have the ".csv" ending.

JSON

A popular data storage format often used by web apps. It's more free-form than CSV, allowing data objects that are nested inside *other* objects. For instance, a "person" object could contain "name" and "age" data, as well as a "pet" object (which has its own "name" and "age.")

XML

Another text-based data storage format. Like HTML, it stores and organizes data using tags, and like JSON, it allows nesting.

Software development

To talk like a software developer, you need to know these common terms and buzzwords. Let's break them down.

A/B tests

Running experiments to decide which features to put into a product, usually a web-based one. You show some users one variation of a feature, and other users a different variation. For instance, Amazon could show half its users a red "buy now" button and the other half a blue button. Then they'd look at various metrics, like the number of sales or number of clicks, to decide which variation is better, and they'd roll out the winning variation to all users. Product managers and developers love A/B testing, since it helps them scientifically determine how to improve their software.

Agile

A software development paradigm that emphasizes short, alternating bursts of writing software and getting feedback from users. For example, instead of taking months or years to release one huge final product, an Agile team would prioritize quickly releasing a "minimum viable product," or a simple prototype. Then the team would get feedback from users to "iterate on" and improve the prototype, repeating this process many times until it is happy with the result.

Angular

Google's web development framework for building web apps. Several popular websites, like Tesla, Nasdaq, and The Weather Channel, use Angular.[3]

Backend

The "behind-the-scenes" part of an app or website that users don't see. The backend stores data, keeps track of users and their passwords, and prepares the webpages that are eventually shown to the user. An analogy: in a restaurant, the cooks in the kitchen are the "backend," since they prepare the food that customers enjoy, even if the customers never see them.

Beta

A preliminary version of software, often released to testers to get user feedback before the final product launches.

Big data

Working with huge amounts of data to extract interesting insights. There's no specific definition of how big counts as "big", but if a dataset is too huge to fit on a single normal-sized computer, there's a good chance that it counts as "big."[4]

Blockchain

The technology behind Bitcoin, blockchain allows for decentralized transactions. Imagine you could hail an Uber without having to use the Uber app or send someone a message without a company like Facebook or your cell phone provider getting in between. With blockchain, everyone shares a record of every past interaction, so you don't need a central authority. With Bitcoin, every user has a list of every past sale, so no one person or company "owns" Bitcoin. This also protects against fraud, since everyone knows if one person is trying to pull something shady.

Bootstrap

A popular toolkit for designing websites, Bootstrap is basically a giant CSS file that contains nicely-designed layouts, fonts, and colors for buttons, headings, and other pieces of webpages. Many websites use Bootstrap as a starting point for their styling; it's a very powerful website template.

Caching

Storing information in a particular place on a computer so you can access it more quickly. It's like storing your favorite pizza place's phone number in your contacts so you don't have to Google it every time — it makes recalling the information faster.

Cookie

Small notes that websites store on your browser to remember information about you. For instance, an e-commerce site could store your cart, preferred language, or username in cookies. Cookies also enable targeted advertising: websites can pass around your location and other personal information via cookies to figure out what you like and hence what ads to show you.

Database

A giant table used to store information; like a superpowered Excel file. For instance, Facebook might store information about all its users in a database, with a separate row for each user and columns for name, birthday, hometown, etc.

Docker

A way for developers to package up everything an app needs to run in a "container," which anyone can run on any supported machine. It's convenient because you don't have to worry about having the right computer configuration; the same container will run the exact same way everywhere. Docker is much more efficient than the alternative, which is to boot up a whole new operating system to run each app.

Flat design

A minimalistic design trend, where you remove unnecessary shiny colors, shadows, animations, and other details, reducing the app to simple colors, geometric shapes, and grids. A few examples are Microsoft's Metro UI (the tiled design used in Windows 8 and 10)[5] and Apple's flattening of iOS since version 7.[6]

Frontend

The user-facing part of a website or app. The frontend includes all the buttons, pages, and pictures that users interact with. It takes information from the user, sends it to the backend, and updates what the user sees once the backend responds. As an analogy, the waiters in a restaurant are the "frontend." Waiters take diners' requests to the cooks (the backend) and serve diners the completed food.

GitHub

A website that hosts millions of open-source software projects. Anyone can see and build on others' code here. Code on GitHub is organized into repositories, or "repos." People can "fork" these repos to make their own versions of the code, and developers can suggest changes to repos using "pull requests."

Hackathon

A coding competition where developers team up to build cool, creative software in short sprints, usually from 12 to 72 hours. Hackathons often feature high-tech prizes, tech company recruiters, free swag like t-shirts and stickers, and late-night food.

Hadoop

A free "big data" software package for storing and analyzing huge amounts of data — we're talking terabytes and petabytes.

jQuery

One of the most famous web development libraries, jQuery is a JavaScript tool that makes interactive websites much easier to build.

Library

A reusable chunk of code that one developer publishes online for other developers to use. For instance, D3 is a famous library that lets JavaScript developers make interactive graphs, charts, and maps with just a few lines of code. *Also known as package or module.*

Linux

A free, open-source family of operating systems; alternatives to Windows and macOS. Many of the world's biggest supercomputers, as well as most web servers, run Linux. Android is built on Linux, too.

Material design

Google's design framework used for Android and many Google apps. It features bright colors, square "cards" of information, and sliding animations. It's similar to flat design, but it has some shadows, gradients, and 3D elements that flat design wouldn't have.[7]

Minification

A technique that developers use to compress their code files by removing any unnecessary bits of text. *Also known as uglification or compression.*

Mockup

After wireframing and prototyping, designers make mockups, which are high-quality drawings that specify exactly which fonts, colors, pictures, spacing, etc. the developers making the app should use. Mockups help designers ensure every detail is perfect and get feedback before the app is actually coded. As UXPin says, "Wireframes are the skeleton. Prototypes demonstrate the behavior. Mockups are the skin."[8]

Node.js

A JavaScript framework for building the backend of web apps.

Open-source

A philosophy for building software where anyone can see, copy, and improve the code behind an app. (It's as if a restaurant let you see the recipes behind its dishes and suggest new ones.) Many popular apps and platforms are open source, like Linux, Android, Firefox, and WordPress.[9] Many programming languages and software development tools are also open-source.[10]

Persona

Example people that designers create to summarize the types of users in their market. Personas have names, backstories, and personalities.[11] For example, LinkedIn's personas could be Sanjana the Student, Ricky the Recruiter, or Jackie the Job-Hunter.

Prototype

An early version of an app or website that lets app makers test their ideas with users. Prototypes can be as complex as clickable websites or as simple as stacks of sticky notes.

React

Facebook's web development framework for building web apps. Websites like Facebook, Instagram, Spotify, The New York Times, Twitter, and many others use React.[12]

Responsive web design

Making websites work well on all screen sizes — phones, tablets, laptops, etc. For instance, the New York Times might show several columns of text on bigger screens (and the print paper), but just one column on smaller screens.

Ruby on Rails

A framework for building web apps using Ruby. Airbnb, Twitch, and Square are all built with Ruby on Rails.[13] *Also known as RoR or Rails.*

Scrum

An offshoot of the Agile method, where software development teams release new features every few weeks, organizing their work into "sprints." They often have daily 15-minute "stand-up" meetings so everyone knows what everyone else is doing and so vital information gets shared across the whole team.

Server

Computers that power websites and many apps. Servers tend not to have screens, touchpads, microphones, or other gadgets. (Most don't even have keyboards and must be programmed remotely!) Instead, they're used solely for their computational might and gargantuan hard drives.

Stack

The suite of technologies that an app or website is built with. This includes the app's choice of frontend tools, backend tools, and database. As an analogy, a car's "stack" could include a particular kind of upholstery, engine, tires, and headlights, among other things.

Terminal

A text-based interface available on computers; developers use the terminal to build software. Even if you're not writing code, the terminal is handy for complex customization, and a few apps can only be run from the terminal, not from the point-and-click interface we're used to. *Also known as command line, shell, or Bash.*

Unix

A family of operating systems including Linux and macOS.

Wireframe

A simple way to draw the "skeleton" of an app or website,[14] like how you might make an outline before writing an essay. Wireframes are made of just lines on paper: buttons and images become boxes, sidebars become rectangles, text becomes squiggly lines, and so on. Wireframes help figure out where page elements should go before anything gets coded.[15]

Technology's alphabet soup

Acronyms might just be the most frustrating part of software jargon. Here are a couple of the most common ones.

AJAX

A method for one website to access information from another using an API. Uses JavaScript.

API

Application Programming Interface: A way for one app to get information from another app, or make another app do something. For instance, Twitter has an API that lets another app post Tweets on someone's behalf, and ESPN has an API that lets you grab the latest sports scores.

AWS

Amazon Web Services: a platform that lets you store data or run apps in the cloud.

CDN

Content Delivery Network: a way for websites to serve images, CSS files, and other "static" assets faster by using a separate dedicated website. These dedicated CDN websites are specialized for holding files instead of running code, and they have many servers scattered around the world, so anyone can get the files much faster than normal.

CPU

Central Processing Unit: the "brain" of a computer or phone, which runs the operating system and apps.

FTP

A protocol for sending files to and from web servers.

GPU

Graphics Processing Unit: a special part of a computer optimized for drawing graphics. If you ever hear the term "hardware-accelerated animation," that uses the GPU.

HTTP

HyperText Transfer Protocol: a protocol used to view webpages on the internet. By "protocol," we mean a set of rules for how information should be transferred.

HTTPS

HyperText Transfer Protocol Secure: an encrypted version of HTTP, which is used for secure online communications like banking, payments, email, and logging into websites.

IaaS

Infrastructure-as-a-Service: tools that let you rent out another company's server space to run your app. One example is Amazon Web Services.[16]

IDE

Integrated Development Environment: a specialized app that makes it easy for developers to build particular kinds of software. Eclipse, for instance, is an IDE for Java and Android. It's like how chefs have their own specialized kitchens with particular tools and ingredients.

I/O

Input/Output: the process of reading and writing files. It's become almost synonymous with tech, to the point where many startups use the ".io" domain ending.

IP

Internet Protocol: a protocol for moving "packets" of information from one computer to another over the internet. Works closely with TCP. HTTP is built on top of TCP and IP.[17]

MVC

Model-View-Controller: A way of organizing code, which often builds on Object-Oriented Programming. Many web or app development frameworks use MVC.

MVP

Minimum Viable Product: in Agile, an early-stage prototype used for early testing. For instance, consider the MVP of the online shoe seller Zappos. The founders took photos of shoes at local stores and posted them on a website — and whenever someone "purchased" a shoe, the founders would buy the shoe from the store and mail it to them.[18] An MVP is just a simple, early version of an app to see if people like the idea.

NLP

Natural Language Processing: a form of artificial intelligence that deals with understanding human languages.

NoSQL

A way of constructing databases, an alternative to (you guessed it) SQL. NoSQL emphasizes more free-form interaction with data rather than just working with rows and columns, which SQL does.

OOP

Object Oriented Programming: a way of structuring code so it's easier to understand, reuse, and build on. You represent everything as an object, from interface elements like *Button* or *Picture* to concepts like *Customer* or *Dog*. For instance, Snapchat could have objects like *User*, *Snap*, *Group*, *Sticker*, *Story*, or *CameraButton*. Each object has its own associated information and actions; for instance, a *Dog* could know its name and know how to bark.

PaaS

Platform-as-a-Service: tools that run an app for you; you just need to send them your code.[19] Between IaaS and SaaS in terms of complexity.

RAM

Random-Access Memory: a computer's "short-term" memory, which apps use to store temporary information like which browser tabs you have open. The more RAM your device has, generally, the faster it is.

REST

A popular type of API. APIs of this type are called RESTful.

ROM

Read-Only Memory: information that's burned onto hardware and usually can't be changed. Computers store the code needed to start the computer in ROM. *Also known as firmware.*

SaaS

Software-as-a-Service: software that's delivered over the internet, meaning you'll often use it in your web browser. Google Docs is a classic example. You'll often need to pay for SaaS apps on a monthly or yearly basis instead of paying to download the app upfront.

SDK

Software Development Kit: a pack of tools that help developers build apps for a particular platform, such as Android or Google Maps.

SEO

Search Engine Optimization: changing your website so it shows up higher in Google search results. One example is including the right keywords in your page's title or headings.

SHA

A popular cryptography algorithm used for encoding and decoding secure communications. There are multiple versions of SHA; as of the time of writing, the most modern one is SHA-3.[20]

TCP

Transmission Control Protocol: a protocol for breaking information into smaller chunks, so you can send it over the internet more easily.

TLD

A domain name ending, such as .com, .org, or .gov. Each country has its own TLD, called a "ccTLD": France has .fr, Mexico has .mx, India has .in, and so on.

TLS

Transport Layer Security: a method of encrypting information sent over the internet so hackers can't snoop on communications. Used in HTTPS.

UI

User Interface: a type of design focusing on making apps and websites look good. Deals with colors, fonts, layout, etc. Often paired with UX.

URL

Uniform Resource Locator: A webpage's address, such as "https://maps.google.com"   or "https://en.wikipedia.org/wiki/Llama".

UX

User Experience: a type of design focusing on making apps and websites easy to use. Deals with how to arrange parts of a website and webpage. Often paired with UI.

Business side

Not to be outdone by the software developers, tech companies' businesspeople — think marketers and strategists — have their own favorite jargon.

B2B

Business-to-business: companies that normally sell to other businesses instead of to average people like you or us. Some famous B2B tech companies are IBM, which sells cloud computing services to businesses, and Accenture, which provides technical consulting.[21]

B2C

Business-to-consumer: companies that sell to consumers; in other words, you could buy their stuff from stores or websites. For instance, Fitbit, Nike, and Ford are B2C. Some companies could be both B2B and B2C. For instance, Coca-Cola sells soda to shoppers but also to universities, hotels, and restaurants.[22] And Microsoft sells Office to both consumers and large businesses.

Bounce rate

How often visitors to your app or website leave without doing anything meaningful, such as clicking a link. A high bounce rate might suggest that visitors aren't interested in what the website has to offer.

Call-to-action (CTA)

A button or link that prompts visitors to take some action, like "Join our mailing list" or "Register for our conference."[23]

Churn rate

The percent of users that a company loses over a particular timespan. For instance, if 1,000 people signed up for

Office 365 but only 750 renewed their subscription the next year, the churn rate would be 25%.

Cost-Per-Click (CPC)

A common type of internet ad, such as the ones seen on Google, that charge advertisers a small fee every time someone clicks on their ads. Also known as Pay-Per-Click (PPC).

Cost-Per-Mille (CPM)

A type of internet ad. Advertisers pay a flat fee each time 1000 people view the ad on a website, such as in Google search results. Also known as Pay-Per-Impression (PPI).

Click-through rate (CTR)

The number of people who clicked on an ad divided by the number of people who saw it and had the option to click on it. In other words, this is the likelihood that an average person would click on the ad. It's a way to measure how successful an ad was.

Conversion

Whenever a user does something that the business wants; the precise action can depend on the company's goals. Conversions could include joining the mailing list, signing up for an account, or buying an item.

Customer Relationship Management (CRM)

Software that a company uses to track its relationships with customers and business partners. Companies can track emails, meeting notes, and other data with CRM software.[24]

Funnel

A metaphor for how the pool of potential customers shrinks before they make a particular "conversion," like buying a product. For instance, suppose an e-commerce website gets 1,000 visitors, but only 500 search for something, 100 put something in their cart, and 50 make a purchase.

Key Performance Indicator (KPI)

A metric that companies use for tracking success of products, teams, or employees. For instance, YouTube's KPIs could include number of users, number of videos, or number of video watches.

Landing page

A small webpage targeted at a particular demographic; it'll often offer visitors something useful like an e-book or mailing list in exchange for their contact information. In marketing-speak, it's a targeted way to acquire "leads."[25]

Lead

Someone who's shown interest in using a service or buying a product. Marketers try to turn strangers into leads and leads into customers, a process called "inbound marketing."[26]

Lifetime value (LTV)

How much money a customer will bring you, directly or indirectly, over the duration of your relationship with them. For instance, if a college bookstore thinks that students will spend $500 a year on textbooks over 4 years of school, each student's lifetime value would be $2,000. Generally, companies will only try to acquire a customer if their lifetime value is higher than the cost of turning them into a customer (known as customer acquisition cost, or CAC).[27]

Market penetration

How much of a target market a product or industry actually reaches. For instance, there are about 30 million teenagers in the US,[28] and if a teen-focused social network had 6 million teenaged users, it'd have 20% penetration of the teenager market.

Market segmentation

Breaking down a huge, diverse market into smaller, more specific ones. For instance, a company could segment its market by gender, location, interests (also known as "psychographics"), and income (part of so-called "behavioral" segmentation).[29]

Net Promoter Score (NPS)

A metric that measures customer satisfaction. Customers are asked to rate a product or service on a scale from 0 (they hate it) to 10 (they love it).[30]

Return on Investment (ROI)

The ratio of a project's profit to its cost.[31] For instance, if you spent $2,000 on an ad campaign and sold $2,600 of extra software as a result, your ROI would be 30%. ROI is just a way to measure "bang for your buck."

Small- and medium-sized businesses (SMBs)

Generally, businesses with under 1,000 employees.[32]

Value proposition

A short statement that explains why consumers would find a product useful. For instance, in 2015 the e-book website Scribd used the value proposition "Read like you own every book in the world."[33]

Year-over-year (YoY)

The change in a metric between a given point and a year earlier. This is useful when there are seasonal variations in the metric. For instance, if educational software sales are always low in summer, it doesn't make sense to compare this June's sales to this March's. Instead, you'd compare to last June's.

Roles at tech companies

Tech companies hire "normal" kinds of professionals, like marketers, CEOs, and HR representatives. But software is made differently than most physical goods, so tech companies have special kinds of roles. Here's a quick glimpse inside the roles in the software industry.

Backend engineer

Software engineers that handle databases and web servers. For instance, Facebook's backend engineers write the code that lets Facebook's supercomputers store billions of photos and handle billions of daily visitors. *See also software engineer.*

Data scientist

Data scientists analyze the company's data (on customers, sales, usage, etc.) to inform the company's business strategy and products.

Designer

Designers make apps and websites beautiful and functional, and they also design stuff like logos, colors, and branding. There are many kinds of designers: UI, UX, visual, motion, and so on.

Frontend engineer

Software engineers who build the customer-facing apps and websites. For instance, Facebook's frontend engineers make the Facebook website and apps look good and work well. *See also software engineer.*

Product Manager (PM)

PMs sit at the intersection of business, design, and engineers. Based on what the customers and business need, PMs decide what products (apps, websites, or hardware) to make and what features the products need to have, then work with engineers to build and launch the products. Think of them as the conductors of the orchestra: they help all the various parts work together to make a great piece of music (or software, in this case).

Product Marketing Manager (PMM)

A slightly more marketing-focused version of Product Managers, they're more focused on launching and marketing products instead of building them.

Quality Assurance engineers (QA)

These engineers rigorously test software and hardware to hunt down bugs and ensure the software is robust.

Software engineer

People who write code and build out software. *Also known as SWE, software developer, or dev.*

Acknowledgements

Very soon after we started writing *Swipe to Unlock*, we realized that we couldn't do it alone — it takes a village, as they say. Here, we'd like to thank all our friends and family who provided their support, feedback, and inspiration as we were writing this book.

Neel

Thanks a million to Alaisha Sharma, Amy Zhao, Andrea Chen, Aron Szanto, Arpan Sarkar, Ivraj Seerha, Jeffrey He, Maitreyee Joshi, Menaka Narayanan, Saim Raza, Sathvik Sudireddy, Sohum Pawar, Tara Mehta, and Vishal Jain for your suggestions and advice on *Swipe to Unlock*. All my other friends deserve a shout-out for putting up with me talking nonstop about this book. I'd also like to thank some of my mentors who have inspired me to use my tech skills to make a difference: Jeff Meisel, Nick Sinai, and William Greenlaw, to name just a few. My fantastic co-authors, Adi and Parth, have been some of the best friends and colleagues. And finally, I'd like to thank my parents for their endless support through whatever I do.

Parth

A huge thank you is in order for all the friends and family who helped us get this book to where it is today. I'd like to especially thank Michelle Wang, Deborah Streeter, Jeremy Schifeling, Jack Keeley, Christina Gee, Stephanie Xu, Niketan Patel, Kevin Cole, Bradley Miles, Ivy Kuo, Krishna Detroja, Gabrielle Ennis, Adam Harrison, Winny Sun, Amanda Xu, William Stern, Samantha Haveson, Suleyman Demirel, and Soundarya Balasubramani. These kind individuals provided their valuable time, skills, opinions, and insights on everything from content to design to marketing. I am incredibly grateful for having the support of such amazing friends and family.

Adi

I would like to thank everyone who patiently helped us along the way — we wouldn't have been able to do it without your support. First, a sincere thank you to Pam Silverstein, Peter Cortle, Professor Nancy Chau, and Professor Michael Roach who enthusiastically encouraged us to share our technology knowledge. Next, I'd like to thank all my friends who helped with everything from reviewing chapters to looking over cover designs — thanks Michelle Jang, Lauren Stechschulte, Holly Deng, Eunu Song, Sai Naidu, Sandeep Gupta, Nivi Obla, Jenny Kim, Brian Gross, Eric Johnson, and Eileen Dai. Also, a huge shout-out to Natsuko Suzuki who tirelessly helped out with the design heavy lifting for the book cover, website, and other branding. And finally, thanks to my family for their support and love throughout this journey.

Index

If you want to learn more about a particular company, app, technology, or concept, here's where you'll find the appropriate pages.

Note that page numbers next to a specific product, such as Amazon Kindle, indicate sections about those products. Page numbers next to a company name indicate sections that are about the company in general, like how Amazon makes money.

Notes

There's so much to know about technology and business strategy, and in *Swipe to Unlock* we've only scratched the surface. That's why we're providing links to every single source we referenced in the book.

To keep the paperback slim, we've put the links on our website at swipetounlock.com/notes/3.4.0. If a particular fact or opinion piques your interest, we encourage you to read the source and dive deeper into the material!